Pilots and Soldiers o[illegible]

Fighting men of the Caribbean

In Memory of my father, who gave me
the inspiration to write this book.
For my mother and daughter,
who have supported me to this end.

For all the men and women of the
Caribbean who fight for Britain

Maureen Dickson

First published in 2020 by

Publishing Push

ISBN paperback: 978-1-8380127-4-8
ISBN ePub: 978-1-8380127-5-5

Contents

Acknowledgements

Richard Melman – TV Commissioning Editor
Simon Painton- ITV Director
Grant Rodgers – Imperial War Museum
Charles Heath Saunders
Peter Devitt
Leroy Gittens
Sharon Devonish
Suffrona Neblett
Julia DeCastro
Samie M. Grant
Nicola Z. Cross
Jan R. Towers
Squadron Leader Ulric Cross, DSO DFC

Who encouraged me from the beginning and never lost faith with what I was trying to do.

My Journey

Pilots and Soldiers of the Caribbean, (Fighting men of the Caribbean) is a celebration of the Caribbean servicemen and women, and their impressive achievements against adversity, discrimination, lack of acknowledgement, racism and rejection.

The idea for this book came to life after having a conversation with my father. He had just turned eighteen years old as the war ended, and was born and raised in what was then known as British Guiana, (now known as Guyana) which is situated in the north of South America, sandwiched between Venezuela and Suriname, (which was formerly known as Dutch Guiana).

Before my father passed, I asked him what his childhood was like and how World War II had affected him and those in Guyana. He said, "As a child, life in Guyana was rather easy-going. From about the age of ten years, I can remember some things of my surroundings, the war years, and the scarcity of many things that were in short supply. My school days were happy ones, and ones I enjoyed very much, and as a teenager, there was always something to do, somewhere to go, and the people were all friendly. You didn't have to know them. You met them on the streets, in the shops, or wherever, and before you knew it, you were chatting away like old friends. I was too young to participate in the war however, some of my older friends and their siblings were old enough and did".

By all accounts, according to my father, his friends were full of enthusiasm. Most of them worked at the same company that my father would later join to do his apprenticeship. As engineers and having a trade, these young men saw themselves as people who had something to offer; most of all they believed that they were going to make a difference. Sadly, many did not return after the war ended, having paid the ultimate price.

This affected the country and its people greatly. Families lost their youngest and brightest who, in most cases, were the breadwinners. Economically, the country was unable to support itself efficiently with the food it produced, due to having to export it to the UK. Although they were suffering, most felt that in some small way they were helping the war effort in Europe.

This meant that the population was given food stamps in order to deal with the shortages not only of certain foods but other commodities such as cotton and certain types of clothing, as they had been exported to Britain to help the population there. This left the people in Guyana having to make do with whatever they could find.

After the war, in the '50s, England looked to the Caribbean again for help. It needed to rebuild the country and needed skilled men and women workers. Armed with his food stamps, my father travelled to

England to answer the call for help. By now, he was a qualified engineer and teacher within his trade, so he was of great value.

The plan for most people who immigrated from the Caribbean in the '50s was that they would stay for five years and then return to their country of origin; my father was no different, except he had planned to later move on to America, where he also had prospects of a good job. For many, including my father, that did not happen. They stayed and helped to build the economy in Britain in the 50s and 60s and beyond. Their children and their children had children, who became fully-fledged British citizens.

As a child, I grew up in England in a climate where the only history I knew was English history. This was no different from what the children of the West Indies or Guiana were taught. It felt quite natural to me, and so there was never a question about my blackness or where I came from, or the fact that there was no one like me in positions of power. As a child/teenager, I believed that I could be whatever I wished to be once I studied and obtained a profession, which I did.

It was not until I became an adult and in my 50s that the penny really started to drop, and I began to realize how uninformed I was about what was going on around me, and that there was a generation of people whose lives and stories had been lost to history, a generation of which I was part. I am sure that I am not the only person who lived in that vacuum; however, it was with that in mind that my journey began.

The descendants of the men and women of WWI and WWII from the West Indies are still fighting for Britain today. For example, my niece joined the Army and served in Bosnia. After returning from several tours of duty in Bosnia and other theatres of war, she returned home and served in the police force before retraining and becoming a barrister.

My research took me to various locations in the UK and the West Indies. I met various dignitaries not only in the Army, Air Force, and Navy, but Prime Ministers, academics, historians, writers, and people in the media.

This book has accounts from Caribbean servicemen and women, not only from WWI and WWII who are no longer with us, but others from consequent conflicts whom I personally interviewed.

I have endeavoured to report the words and feelings of the "Fighting men and women of the Caribbean" and their experiences, as they have related them to me, as factually as I can and without prejudice.

Why does it matter to tell this story?

- There is little known of the fighting men and women of the Caribbean, who left their own country (some at a very early age), to travel thousands of miles to join the services. Although their motives were varied, the bottom line was that they were fighting to keep democracy alive.

Most were fighting for the mother country, for Britain.

- Generations of children and adults alike grew up unaware of this contribution, as those who are left who fought in the war are now but a few. There is so little that is documented about them that the same photos and stories are told over time immemorial. Therefore, every account and book written about them should count.
- The book aims to give recognition to a unique history and untold stories that deserve to be heard and to give the soldiers and RAF personnel a voice.

Role Models

It is said that black children in Britain today have no role models; however, this is untrue, there are role models out there.

The fact is they have not been brought to our attention, mainly in the beginning for reasons to do with the empire and political issues.

There are many well-educated Caribbean heroes of WWI and WWII who fought for Britain.

In secondary school in the West Indies, most of the navigators and pilots were taught to write and speak Latin and some Greek, as was the case for Ulric Cross, who did both. These were men and women from the Caribbean who were determined to make a difference to assist Britain, and they succeeded despite all the obstacles placed in their way. At the end of the day, 103 medals had been awarded by the end of WWII.

These men, in particular, were not made by the RAF, Army or Navy. They already had the potential to be great men. This is demonstrated by the fact that many of those who survived the wars became: -

actors, writers, jet pilots, barristers, teachers, ministers, high court judges, commercial pilots,

> CEOs of large corporations, attorney generals to various countries, the first black mayor of Lambeth, and one became owner of an airport, (Gatwick), which is used by many of us at one time or another.

These men are some of our role models and had the drive and the intelligence to achieve, but were pushed into the background and ignored. However, they had the determination to succeed and did, and for that reason, we are speaking about them today.

The Caribbean

The Commonwealth Caribbean is the term applied to the English-speaking islands in the Caribbean Sea and the mainland nation of Belize (formerly British Honduras), also known as the West Indies. Guyana, (formerly British Guiana), is the only South American country which was once colonised by the British and is part of the Commonwealth, and as such, is sometimes clubbed together with the West Indies, especially in sport, such as the West Indian cricket team. The rest of the Caribbean, as it is known, is in the Caribbean Sea.

The Caribbean Sea

Throughout its history, the Caribbean has alternated between extremes of war and peace, wealth and poverty, tension and repose. For centuries, the Caribbean had been a place of explosive violence, where Amerindians, Spaniards, Frenchmen, Dutchmen, English, and pirates of many nations fought for control of its resources. For a time, its islands were one of the wealthiest places on Earth, and the quarrels of far-off Europe were played out in its straits and bays and islands. In time, the "West Indian" became the term that described those who lived on the islands of the Greater and Lesser Antilles – of all races, and in time, ships were no longer laden with silver and gold.

The West Indian Islands sat astride a sea lane that leads from the Atlantic to the Pacific through the Panama Canal, and was four thousand miles from the land in Europe, but linked both theatres of war in both oceans. This meant that they were in a position to protect the busy American ports along the Gulf of Mexico more significantly, they controlled the traffic between Britain and a very important source of oil, which came from Venezuela via the refineries of Aruba, Curacao and Trinidad. In addition, Guyana provided vital supplies of sugar and bauxite (aluminium ore) which was used for the manufacturing of planes during the war. These things made the region an obvious target and they did not go unnoticed by the Germans or their submarines in WWII.

Empire

At the height of the Empire, Britain held a vast amount of land, countries, and people, spreading its language, customs, and identity, while convincing the indigenous people that they were British too.

When war broke out across Europe, things started to change because the colonies began to see and realise that they were not truly accepted as British and that Britain and its people were no different from them.

This was borne out by the beginning of change and the erosion of the Empire, which Britain had tried so hard to hold on to. After previously telling them that Britain was the "Mother Country", the British began discouraging people from travelling there or participating in the war as they privately considered the war to be a "white man's war", something that was voiced at one time by its leaders.

Due to obstacles the Caribbean volunteers faced, some travelled to Canada or France where things were better and they were able to join up in some capacity in order to participate in the upcoming war effort.

As far back as 1836, Britain transported indentured slaves from East India to Guyana. The population of

Guyana included its own indigenous Indians. However, the importation of these foreign labourers from India, China and Gibraltar, to mention a few, to Guyana, Trinidad & Tobago, meant that the dynamics of these countries were changed. This caused division in the host country, so much so that, particularly in Guyana, division in the parliamentary system remains today.

Without realising it, Britain had laid down the roots in the colonies for discontent and the break-up of the Empire. By the 1960s, most of Britain's territories had become independent countries.

In this book there are many acts of racism, however, for every act of racism somewhere, there was acceptance, kindness, and understanding. The book is not about racism, but about the way in which it has affected us all, and in time of war. It aims to demonstrate how Caribbean men and women in the services put their difficulties aside in order to fight for a country they believed to be worth fighting for, and for which some paid the ultimate price. Who will remember them?

Although there were those who held on to racism and separation as part of the Empire, others were willing to embrace change and the inevitability that, with all of the people of its colonies, who it had ruled over for so long, landing on its shores, Britain was becoming a multi-cultural country.

The Service in WWI

Britain's declaration of war on Germany was on the 4th of August 1914. It was triggered by events leading to the assassination of Archduke Ferdinand and quickly spread globally. The Caribbean countries were directly affected due to their colonial connections with Britain. Jamaica, in particular, saw Britain as the "Mother Country", and started to make moves to establish a regiment to fend off a possible German invasion. However, this was not straightforward.

There had been a regiment called the West India Regiment (WIR), which was a part of the infantry regiment, made up of a small number of Europeans, West Indians and some colonies of the Caribbean between 1795 and 1927. The black soldiers, who were initially recruited, were slaves from the plantations in the West Indies.

The regiment saw considerable service in the Napoleonic Wars. Today, on Nelson's column in Trafalgar Square, a black serviceman can be seen on one of the friezes on the side pointing to where the shot came from that killed Nelson. After the Mutiny Act was passed in parliament in 1807, all the soldiers who were recruited as slaves in the WIR were freed. On the outbreak of WWI, recruits were volunteers from the WIR, but the senior NCOs were white and came from England.

Although this was the case, the British War Office initially opposed the recruitment of West Indian troops into the ranks; it went so far as to include institutional racism in its Army manual of military laws. The classification in the manual stated that "black men" or "men of colour" should be considered as aliens, thus, restricting the numbers that could be allowed into the service. This was used as a form of colour bar.

When it looked as if the Germans were infringing on the West Indies, which would have jeopardised Britain's interests and supplies of oil, cotton, and other commodities, King George gave the go-ahead to form a new regiment called the British West Indies Regiment (BWIR), in order to serve overseas, unlike the WIR, which was formed in the West Indies to defend their own islands on behalf of British interests.

Part of an Advertisement on Behalf of King George V Calling Men to Fight

'The British Empire is engaged in a life-and-death struggle. Never in the history of England, never since the misty distant past of 2,000 years ago, has our beloved Country been engaged in such a conflict as she is engaged in today.

HIS MOST GRACIOUS MAJESTY KING GEORGE has called on the men of the Empire, MEN OF EVERY CLASS, CREED, AND COLOUR, to COME FORWARD TO FIGHT.

This call is to YOU, young man! Not your neighbour, not your brother, not your cousin, but YOU!'

Recruitment for the Regiment started in 1915; however, they were not allowed the same rights or seen as equals alongside white soldiers, as they were considered to be unintelligent and not able to follow what the War Office thought were intricate orders, and were not disciplined enough. To this end, they appointed a white Officer to take charge. There was also the fear that now, holding a gun in their hands, the soldiers might kill white men; this was not acceptable even in battle at the time, as there was a worry that it would affect the image of the Empire.

In the English camps, the regiment ran into difficulties against them, not by their fellow soldiers, but by the military authorities, who denied them a pay rise at one time, while their white comrades received theirs. It was only given after protests from various island governments and some serving soldiers, that led to them eventually being given the increase.

The British West Indies Regiment arrived in the winter of 1915 for military training at North Camp in

England; they were the first contingent who came from Trinidad, Grenada, and Barbados.

The ships they were travelling on were diverted to Halifax, Canada. The clothes they were wearing were not suitable for the weather. This caused hundreds of the men to suffer from severe frostbite. They were sent back to the West Indies as unfit to serve without even reaching England. As men discharged as unfit, they were not considered entitled to any benefits or pensions, and so became destitute, while the few who were entitled experienced excessively long delays before they received assistance. On their arrival home, they found that they could not find work as they had already relinquished their jobs in order to fight for King and Country.

When the war became intense at the Battle of the Somme, and the army experienced large numbers of casualties among the fighting white troops, reinforcements were needed on the front line, so the black troops were summoned up in a supporting role. Later, it was decided that the Regiment should be sent to Egypt to fight the Turks or used to garrison the West African territories captured from Germany. However, their white comrades were exempt from going.

While in Salonika, Mesopotamia, and Egypt, they were made to work for the general public, and used as dockworkers. Many had no leave since enlisting as much as three years earlier. It got to a point where they had suffered enough and so refused to work, and demanded that their white officers be removed and men of colour put in their place. There were also refusals in Canada, as the men wanted to go home since the white soldiers had already gone.

The Regiment had experienced real racism, not only from the British but from the Germans too. There was a story that, while at war, "The Tommie's" British soldiers captured some German prisoners who proceeded to spit on their hands and then wipe them on the faces of the black soldiers, as if to say that they were painted black.

There is evidence, however, of Caribbean soldiers being involved in actual combat in France, where the West Indies Regiment fought off a German assault armed only with knives they had brought from home. They also saw service against the German Cameroons, and the German forces in Mombasa in Kenya, where they were mentioned in despatches and earned eight Distinguished Conduct Medals.

In 1918, The BWIR took part in a successful battle in Palestine, in which two men, Lance corporal Sampson and Private Spence, were awarded the Military Medal for bravery during the action. The Regiment was praised for their work in the highest terms by Major General Sir Edward Clayton.

Although the Regiment had proved their worth, it was a puzzle to most why the Colonial office dispatched an office paper that said that they were found sleeping in hammocks all day and drinking rum, as most of these statements were proved to be untrue.

They were later given "labour duties", such as digging trenches, stretcher-bearing, working in ammunition dumps and gun emplacements, building roads, loading ships and trains and cleaning toilets, but most of all becoming cooks, and man-servants to their white officers.

In 1918, battalions that were sent to Italy were ordered to unload ships and perform other heavy work, some unloading ammunition without the required protective gloves. On 6th December 1918, they had endured enough and hence turned on the few black officers they had at that time, who were following the orders of their superiors and ignoring their complaints.

The soldiers refused to work in protest. 180 sergeants sent a petition to the Secretary of State complaining about the constant discrimination against them, as a result of which they had been denied promotions and a pay increase while being forced to work in poor conditions.

This dispute caused tempers to become frayed and fighting broke out.

In response, the commanders at Taranto dispatched a machine–gun Company to restore order. Perceived ringleaders were rounded up and prison sentences were given out; one of them received a 20-year sentence and another was executed by firing squad. The 9th BWIR was then disbanded in 1920. The men were then distributed to other battalions, which were all subsequently disarmed. Although the mutiny was crushed, the bitterness persisted.

Many returned to the Caribbean, wounded and disillusioned. The sense of injustice was still strong. Over one thousand men had died and more than three thousand wounded. This led to the Caribbean League being formed; its aim was for black men to have their freedom and govern themselves in the West Indies. This eventually led to self-rule and independence.

Regardless of all the hardship that they were presented with, the Caribbean and African men of WWI overcame adversity, (some at the cost of their lives), but they played their part admirably. However, the Empire, and colonialism as we knew it, were ending.

With the start of WWII, yet again there were more hurdles to overcome for the Caribbean volunteers. The RAF, Army and Royal Navy were all reluctant to employ Caribbean service personnel and were always able to find a way in which to exclude them from their particular service. They would add rules and specifications to their documentation, manuals or practices devised to exclude Caribbean men when applicants attempted to join up at their recruitment offices. This is an example of how they justified their actions:

RAF – Remark made by
J. Slessor, Air Member for Personnel, who went on to command the RAF.

"[A man] as black as your hat [whose] name is U-Ba or Ah Wong. ... [A] gentleman who looks as though he had just dropped out of a tree .... is clearly unlikely to make as good

an officer or NCO as an otherwise less highly qualified white man, because the men won't take it from him".
The National Archives, AIR 2/13437 — J. Slessor-minutes from the meeting on 16 August 1945.

The RAF made an announced on the 19th October 1939 by the Colonial Office which said: -
"Non-pure Europeans" would be eligible for temporary commissions in the military during the war. However, 'this does not mean that British subjects who are obviously men of colour will in practice receive commissions... only that the men will not be turned down on "Pure European descent" basis at the recruitment offices.

Comment by the Army during WWII in its official manual.
"Blacks or people of colour should be discouraged from serving".

A Foreign Office memorandum in February 1944 stated: -
"We must keep up the fiction of there being no colour bar, while actually, only those with special qualifications are likely to be accepted".

Army medical officers were given a code which would bring restriction of ethnic minorities into the ranks: -
The Army medical officers were told to use the secret designation of the "D Factor personnel" which was to

single out would-be soldiers with "Asiatic or negroid features". A simple "D" would be placed on the applying soldiers' records, at which point he would be rejected.

This seemed rather unfair since these men were physically fit, well-educated to a very high standard, and were the calibre of other men who were applying to join the British armed services.

David Clemetson

1st October 1893 – 21st September 1918
1st Sportsman's Battalion
The 23rd Battalion, Royal Fusiliers
The 24th Welsh Regiment of the Pembroke Yeomanry

In 1914, a law was written into the Military Manual, that stated: -

> "Any negro or person of colour would not be allowed to hold the rank above sergeant".

Nevertheless, in 1914, David Clemetson, a Jamaican, was allowed in and had been one of the first volunteers. Had he not, it would not have been an issue as men of colour were not wanted in the forces and so subscription did not apply to them, and no one would have thought it untoward if he did not at least attempt to join.

However, by 1915 when the Caribbean's were beginning to arrive in service, he had already been in service for one year and had become a 2nd Lieutenant. This was due, almost certainly, to the fact that he looked white in colour, and because of his background. Clemetson was a 20-year-old law student at Cambridge University when he heard that war had broken out.

In the general scheme of things, Clemetson was not an ordinary person for his time. His family was well known and wealthy. Born in Jamaica, his grandfather, Robert Clemetson had been enslaved but was also the son of his owner, who freed him and left him money. He then became one of the wealthy elites on the island. Due to his inheritance, he also became a slave owner. He became a politician and was elected to the House of Assembly in Jamaica in 1840.

The Clemetson's were light-skinned, and not only wealthy but powerful, and dominated the British colony as part of its elite landowners. They even traded bananas with an Italian American family in Baltimore.

David, who was named after his father, was born in Port Maria, in Saint Mary Parish, Jamaica. He was the eldest son and was educated in Jamaica, and also in Clifton College, Bristol, England, where he served in the Officers' Training Corps, before going on to Trinity

College Cambridge. In 1912, while still at Cambridge, he rowed for the First Trinity Boat Club's fourth boat, which was crewed by the rugby team, which he also belonged to.

David Clemetson had heard it said that the First World War was a "white man's war." However, he wanted to show that people from the colonies like him, who's origin was that of a Jamaican, were willing to fight for King and Country. Although he entered the service in 1914, it was not until 1916 that he had his first participation in the war, in Salonika on the Macedonian line. Now a 2nd Lieutenant, after a stint on the line, he became traumatised and suffered from shell-shock and was evacuated.

The hospital ship that he had boarded to return to Britain was, in turn, torpedoed by a German U-boat. After being rescued, he ended up in a psychiatric hospital for officers in Scotland. On his physical medical report, in the box for 'complexion', the doctor wrote "colour of skin dusky, between light and dark". Clemetson, however, never denied his blackness, although he might have got away with it due to his complexion.

It later transpired that the Forces were recruiting black men with the deciding factor being how light in colour they were. If they had to have a black officer for whatever reason, he had to be light-skinned enough that it would make others think twice before asking the question.

The British Military decided, after being presented with these educated, middle-class, good-looking, light-skinned black men, that it could do no harm turning a blind eye to its own institutionalised racism laws, (although they did not see it as institutional racism as such at the time) if they allowed a handful of black soldiers among them. Hence Clemetson, Tull, and Bemand all became officers, but they all had special attributes. Clemetson came from a wealthy family and studied at Cambridge, Tull was intelligent and a recognised professional footballer and Bemand had a General's approval behind him, and all were nearly as white in appearance.

Putting aside the fact that George Bermand lied about his heritage, he was one whose story came to light through historian Simon Jervis. George Bemand, also a 2nd Lieutenant in the Royal Field Artillery in 1914, lied when asked whether he was of "pure European descent". He said yes, and was accepted, although previously, on a trip to America, he was classed as "African-Black" as his father was white English and his mother Jamaican. This did not mean that these men of fair skin were seen as equals by the British; they were just tolerated.

During his war years, Clemetson also served in Egypt and was killed in action in 1918 near Péronne, France, on the Somme. He was posthumously awarded the Victory Medal and the British War Medal. He is buried in Unicorn Cemetery, Vendhuile, France.

Alhaji Grunshi

Gold Coast Regiment 1918

Alhaji Grunshi's story is one that is still taking place today, in different parts of our society, to people of colour.

Although Alhaji Grunshi was the first black British soldier to fire the first shot in WWI on the 4th August 1914, and was later awarded the Military Medal for bravery in 1918, Grunshi was as much a British subject as anyone, but of course, came from Africa and was black.

History has credited the first shot to a white soldier named Ernest Edward Thomas, a soldier who fired his gun on the 22nd August 1914, 18 days after Grunshi.

It is only with extensive research that it was realised that Grunshi was the first, however, at that time, the fact that he made the first shot, would have, it was felt, questioned the very nature of British identity.

Grunshi was part of The Gold Coast Regiment, which was commanded by white British officers.

Ahmet Ali

Captain - Ahmet Ali Celikten 1883-1969 Pilot Ottoman Aviator

Ahmet Ali Celikten Was the first-ever Black (aviator) military pilot in history. He served with the Ottoman Empire from 1908-1920, and flew as an officer in the Ottoman Empire's Naval Air Service, and participated in World War 1. Turkey was, of course, allied to Germany from November 1914.

He was born Izmirli Ahmet Ali, his mother being Zenciye Emine Hanim and father Ali Bey, who was of African Turkish descent.

His grandmother came from Bornu (now Nigeria) and was enslaved and transported from Africa to the Ottoman Empire, where his mother met and married his father in lzmir, the old capital of the Ottoman Empire, in 1883, and that is where he was born. The Ottoman Empire was founded in 1299 by Oghuz Turks under Osman 1st in north-western Anatolia.

Ahmet flew a Bleriot X1-2 monoplane, a two-seater version of the aircraft in which Louis Bleriot flew across the English Channel in 1909. There is a Bleriot X1 suspended from the roof in the RAF Museum.

Ahmet's ambition was to serve in the Ottoman navy, and in 1904, he was accepted as a cadet by the Naval Technical School. It is interesting that the colour of his skin was apparently no obstacle, whereas a black applicant attempting to join the British armed forces at this time would certainly have been turned down. In 1908, Ahmet passed out from the Technical School as a First Lieutenant.

In 1916, Ahmet won his wings and began his career as a naval aviator. By 18th December 1917, he had reached the rank of Captain and was posted to Berlin, where his brother was killed in battle. After returning from Berlin, he went back to Turkey, spending the rest of the war as a flying and engineering instructor at Yeshilköy.

Ahmet married Hatice Hanim, from Preveza in Greece, and had two daughters. In the 1930s, Ahmet was employed as a civil airline pilot and taught both of his girls to fly.

He had received several honours, including the Bahri Aircraft Medal, and is believed to have been the first pilot of African ancestry, although, in the confusion of time, Eugene Bullard is sometimes given that honour.

Ahmet Ali Celikten, the world's first black military pilot, died in New York City in 1969.

Eugene Bullard
Pilot

Eugene Bullard
Born 9th October 1895
The only African-American to serve as a pilot during World War 1 - He flew for France

The most famous of the black pilots of the First World War was Eugene Bullard, an African-American born in Columbus, Georgia in 1895. Although he was never recognised at the time, and was rejected several times, yet he was loved and revered by the French.

Despite being born in America, he came from part-Caribbean heritage. His father was from Africa and the

French Caribbean country of Haiti, and his mother was Creek Indian.

Eugene was the 7th of 10 children, a number that his father considered very lucky. While growing up, Eugene witnessed white men attempting to lynch his father, while one of his brothers was lynched. The reality of racism in Georgia made Eugene decide to leave America.

His father had always told him that, in France, all men were considered equals. Eugene ran away from home at the age of 16 and ended up wandering around America for a few years, before boarding a German ship that he thought was French. They were very nice to him and taught him German, but they had to let him off at the first port of call, which was Aberdeen in Scotland.

He did several jobs while moving from city to city, one of which was working in a boxing establishment, sweeping the floors at first until he was able to progress and become a boxer in Liverpool. While on a trip to France to box, he decided at the end of the tour he would not return to Scotland, as France was always where he had wanted to be.

When war broke out, he joined the French Foreign Legion and saw action in Picardy and Artois. He then transferred to the crack 170th Infantry Regiment which was sent to fight at the Battle of Verdun in 1916. After being wounded, he was sent back to Paris.

While speaking to friends one day, he mentioned that he thought that he would apply to become a pilot. His friends laughed as no one had heard of a black combat pilot. Eugene applied anyway and was accepted to join the French Air Service and was initially accepted as a gunner, but was selected for flying training and qualified as a pilot on 5th May 1917.

He was posted to the Lafayette Flying Corps of the French Air Service along with over 250 other American volunteers. He was promoted to corporal and was posted to Escadrille N0. 93 in August 1917, and then on to join Escadrille N0. 85 in mid-September.

Although not officially confirmed, he was credited with two aerial victories, and gained the name "The Black Swallow of Death" and wore a dramatic personal emblem of a red heart pierced by a dagger with the legend "All Blood Runs Red" in French.

Bullard certainly cut a dash and an American officer left this vivid impression of the black aviator. He was good-looking, charming, charismatic and clever.

An American Officer once said of Eugene Bullard: -

> **"Suddenly, the door opened to admit a vision of military splendour such as one does not see twice in a lifetime. It was Eugene Bullard... He wore a pair of tan aviator's boots which gleamed with a mirror-like lustre, and above them, his breeches smote the eye with a dash of vivid scarlet. His black tunic, excellently cut and set off by a fine figure, was decorated with a pilot's badge, a Croix de Guerre...and a pair of enormous wings, which left no possible**

> **doubt...as to which arm of the Service he adorned...I repressed a strong instinct to stand at attention."**

In 1917, the United States entered the war and Bullard applied to join the American Air Service. He passed the medical but was refused entry because he was black.

Shortly after this ruling, a disillusioned Eugene was involved in a fight with a French officer while on leave in Paris and was dismissed from the Air Service. However, this did not affect his popularity.

Another fellow American pilot later wrote:

> "There was scarcely an American (on the squadron) who did not know and like Bullard. He was a brave, loyal and a very likeable fellow; with or without withdrawal from Aviation, there was scarcely an American who did not regret the fact" of not having his presence in the service.

In 1918, Bullard returned to the 170th Regiment until discharged from the French Army in 1919. Bullard received no fewer than 15 French decorations, including the Croix de Guerre and the Medaille Militaria.

Bullard returned to Paris and eventually ran his own nightclub called L'Escadrille, where he met Louis Armstrong, Josephine Baker, and the writer, Langston Hughes.

Eugene owned and ran several nightclubs, and so was well-placed when he was asked to become a spy for the French, as many Germans frequented his high-flying clubs, along with famous people of the day. There was also the fact that he spoke and understood German and spoke several other languages. He also volunteered to fight for the French in WWII.

Later, he was awarded a commemorative medal for his service to France in the Second World War. When the Germans invaded France in 1940, Bullard escaped to the United States. Although the Germans invaded Paris in a friendly manner, if you could call invasion friendly, being an intelligence officer, and black, Paris was not the best place for him to be.

In 1949, Bullard attended a concert in Peekskill, New York, by the singer Paul Robeson. There was a mob of local men who attacked the concert-goers and Bullard was badly injured, however, no one was prosecuted for the assault.

In 1954, the French government invited Bullard to a ceremony at the Tomb of the Unknown Soldier at the Arc de Triomphe in Paris, and five years later he was made Chevalier (Knight) of the Legion d'honneur. In 1959, Bullard was interviewed about his experiences by NBC Television. He was, at that time, an elevator operator at the Rockefeller Centre and he chose to wear the Legion d' honneur on his work uniform for the interview.

Eugene Bullard experienced a lot in his relatively short life, not only through moving from country to country to fight, but participating in and surviving some of the most heavily contested battles of WWI, from the battles of the Somme front and Artois Ridge, to Mont-Saint-Eloi, to mention a few. Even when the Germans decided to shoot on the spot any Legionnaires they found, he still managed to outwit them.

He died of stomach cancer in New York on the 12th October 1961 at the age of only 66. He was surrounded by French officers who came to give their respects.

He was buried by the French in their military cemetery with full military honours in the French war veteran's section. He was buried with his "Legion d'honneur" medal (legion of merit) – the highest award that can be given by the French.

Sixty years after his first combat, the Americans granted a motion in the Senate to posthumously award him the title of Second Lieutenant of the United States' Air Force; they decided that, due to his courage and tenacity, it was time they recognised him.

He had been a soldier, combat pilot, spy, welterweight boxer, jazz musician, club owner, gym owner, and civil rights activist, and had married a Countess and had two children.

Unfortunately, he ended his life as a lift assistant in the Rockefeller Centre in New York. However, he did have fifteen minutes of fame when he was discovered by a customer and was invited on "The Today Show" in 1959, where some of his medals, which were many, were displayed on TV.

Today, he is slowly being recognised by Americans, and they are finding out what the French knew all along, that Eugene Bullard was a giant and a hero.

He was nicknamed "Black Swallow of Death", which was also on the side of his plane.

Legion d'honneur, Croix de guerre x2, Croix du combatant volontaire 1914-1918. Insigne des blessés militaires, Medaille Interalliée, Guerre x2, Medaille commemorative de la guerre 1914-18.

These are but a few of the French medals that were bestowed upon this exceptional pilot.

Walter Tull

Born 28th April 1888

First Black Army Officer of WWI

Mixed race heritage

Professional Footballer

Awarded 1914-15 Star & British War Victory medals, which he never received, due to his colour

Walter D. J. Tull was the son of Daniel Tull from Barbados. His mother was English, and her maiden name was Alice Palmer before she married Walter's father.

Alice's mother was born in Folkestone, but she spent most of her life in Hougham, Dover with her farmworker husband, who came from the village. Alice was born to them in March 1853 at Elms Farm, in Dover, known as the "Conker Pond".

Daniel married twice and Walter became one of six children. When Daniel passed, Walter was quite young, about nine years old. His stepmother at this point decided that she had to send Walter and his brother Edward to an East London Orphanage. Eventually, Walter's brother was adopted and lived in Scotland and eventually became a dentist, while Walter stayed in London, and became a professional footballer.

By 1909, Walter was well known, as he played for Tottenham Hotspur FC. Later, in 1911, he played for Northampton Town FC. At this time, there was an incident when Walter was playing in a match at Bristol, that moved a news reporter to say: -

> "Let me tell those Bristol hooligans that Tull is so clean in mind and method as to be a model for all white men who play football... In point of ability, if not in actual achievement, Tull was the best forward on the field."

Walter played for Northampton Town FC until the outbreak of the First World War. He became a 2nd Lieutenant after enlisting into the 17th (1st Football) Battalion of the Middlesex Regiment in 1914.

Walter was recommended for the Military Cross by his superiors for his gallantry and coolness under fire. However, Walter never received his award because of the Army's Military Law, which forbade "any negro or person of colour" being commissioned and so, when the recommendation reached Head Office for action, it was deemed a step too far.

As all Officers at the Somme led from the front, so did Walter. On the 25th March 1918 (a month before his 30th birthday), he led an advance on the German trenches in Favrile, France. As they crossed "no man's land" they were under fire from German machine guns. He was hit and killed, his body never to be found. He was so well-liked by his men that they attempted, under heavy fire, to recover his body.

However, there was too much heavy fire, and they could not reach where they thought he had fallen. It was also said that under that sort of bombardment, the bodies of all the men that fell turned black, so it was difficult to know who was who, and so, they were unable to recover his body for burial.

Like 35,000 others who died in the region and have no known grave, Walter is commemorated on the Arras Memorial.

Several members of parliament have been trying for years to have the medals awarded to him given to him posthumously, however, they have not been successful as yet. He was also the first man of colour to become an outfield professional footballer, and one of the first black officers, if not the first.

Today, Walter is acclaimed with pride as one of Folkstone's famous sons. He is now known as never before, as there have been documentaries and even dramatisations of his story. Britain has now acknowledged him. However, there is still a way to go in regard to obtaining the medals he was awarded and died for.

William Robinson Clarke

William Robinson Clarke
Kingston, Jamaica
1895 - 1981
First black pilot to fly for Britain.

William Robinson Clarke, known as Robbie Clark, was born in Kingston, Jamaica in October 1895. He received a decent education, and his main interest was motor cars, which were a novelty in Jamaica at that time. To follow his interest, he applied for and received a job as a chauffeur and was one of the first men, white or black, to drive on the island.

In 1915, Caribbean men were allowed to join the services. The Royal Flying Corps was the air arm of the British Army, before and during the First World War, until it merged with the Royal Naval Air Service in April 1918, the predecessor of the Royal Air Force.

Clarke joined the Royal Flying Corps on 26th July 1915, and his first job was as a2nd Class Air Mechanic; he was then posted to France as a driver with an observation balloon company.

He never took his eye off the ball in regard to wanting to fly, and in December 1916 he was accepted for pilot training in England.

It took Clarke a year till 26th April 1917 to obtain his wings and the Royal Aero Club aviation certificate. He was then promoted to sergeant and then became a member of 4th Squadron Royal Flying Corps, which was stationed at Abele, Belgium, not far behind the British front lines at Ypres, where fighting had been going on since 1914. At this point, he was the first black Caribbean pilot to fly for Britain. During his flying career, Clarke also flew with 254 Squadron of the Royal Air Force (RAF).

We know a lot of what Robinson Clarke was thinking and experiencing as he wrote letters to his mother and others in which he talked about his experiences. He also sent articles about his exploits in France to the Gleaner Newspaper, one of which was published on 7th September 1917.

Robbie Clarke's flying career did not last long, as was common for most pilots of the time, as in the same year that he received his wings, he was shot down and injured on the 28th July 1917.

Clarke and his observer, Second Lieutenant F.P. Blencowe were flying an RE8 reconnaissance aircraft over the Western Front while taking photographs, when in his letter to his mother he said, “Five Hun scouts come down upon me, and before I could get away, I got a bullet through the spine. I managed to pilot the machine nearly back to the aerodrome but had to put her down as I was too weak to fly anymore; my observer escaped without any injury”.

Clarke was flying his RE8 biplane over the Western Front, over Ypres, five miles onto the German side. After he lost consciousness for a few moments, Clarke managed to fly and land the plane back at the base. Luckily, the observer was not hurt. It had been Clarke’s second ‘scrap’. Robbie was very lucky as there were no parachutes in those days.

Clarke returned to Jamaica after the war. After he recovered from his wounds, he became a builder, and later a Life President of the Jamaican branch of the Royal Air Force’s Association.

Clarke died in April 1981 at the age of 88. He was looked on as a hero, as he had a bullet go through his spine and still managed to fly and land his plane and observer safely on the ground.

William ‘Robbie’ Clarke was awarded the Silver War Badge, was in the battle of Messines, and is buried in Kingston Military Cemetery in Jamaica.

Before the Caribbean Joined WWII

Even though there had been a black regiment in WWI, the West Indian Regiment (WIR), the Caribbean barely featured on the agenda during the 1920s for those in power in Westminster. Instead, there was a lot of infighting, particularly as Lloyd George did not like Winston Churchill and had different ideas as to what should be done in regard to various subjects and situations.

The people of the West Indies were considered part of the British Empire, but the West Indies were only to be considered as a place of plantation agriculture, and a pool from which to obtain cheap labour, which could be exported elsewhere. However, things were changing.

In 1930, when the great depression emerged, although thousands of miles away from Britain and the rest of Europe, it brought hardship to the West indies. Seeing how Britain was in no better position than themselves, and how their fortune was decided by what Britain did, relations began to change. The West Indies decided to put their own house in order themselves, and a new confidence was born. This was done by way of increasing organised labour militancy, driven by trade unions, demanding improved working conditions and rights for workers.

However, they were yet to find their own identity as the Islands were more British than the British. Every schoolchild sang the national anthem, spoke English and knew about the English culture, and its history of kings and queens. Nothing was taught in school about their own country or culture. The Caribbean became a reflection of Britain in many ways.

Preparation for WWII

With the proclamation of WWII and the German activity in the seas around the West Indies and South America, the waters around the Caribbean became a very dangerous place.

Guyana, for example, imported a great deal of its food, such as flour, potatoes, fish and meat, from Canada and the USA, so the Germans targeted the Caribbean shipping lanes, making these commodities scarcer and increasing the cost of living not only in Guyana but throughout the region.

Contributions

- The West Indies and Guyana gave the British Government gifts to the value of several thousands of pounds to the war effort. Below are listed some, but not all of these gifts: -
- 9 Aeroplanes

- 11 Ambulances & adequate funds for their maintenance
- Warships
- Tea Trucks
- Cotton
- Logwood
- Lime
- Rum
- Condensed milk
- Margarine
- Biscuits
- Rice
- Demerara Sugar
- Oil
- Clothing
- Dogwood
- Monetary donations, for instance: -

  British Guiana gave - £128,877
  Barbados - £202.332
  Jamaica - £223,376
  Trinidad & Tobago - £929,095
  Bermuda - £344,133

These amounts may seem small by today's standards; however, we must remember that this was in 1939, and they would have been considered to be large sums and added to the severe hardships to the countries who donated them interest-free, especially when added to that the materials and commodities sent.

The colonies encouraged their people to invest in war bonds. Individuals and voluntary organizations joined together to raise money and materials to send to Britain. There was a buzz in the West Indies and everyone wanted to do their bit.

Many felt that they were helping Britain out as they were part of the British Empire, and were willing to make the sacrifices and to support her with whatever contributions they could make, even though it meant that they went without, and many did.

Start of World War II

From the time the war started in 1939 until its end in 1945, virtually every country in the world was involved, and it is believed that more than 100,000,000 people participated.

Britain introduced conscription; however, this was not the case in the colonies. Around 16,000 West Indians volunteered, many of whom paid to travel to Britain in order to fight alongside the British during the Second World War.

Over 100 were women; 80 chose the WAAF (Women's Auxiliary Air Force) and 30 Joined the ATS (Auxiliary Territorial Service).

Around 6,000 West Indians served with the RAF and Canadian Air Force in roles from pilots, bombers, air gunners, RAF ground crew, to administrators. 236 Caribbean's were killed, 50 of whom joined the RAF and died not long after, and 265 were wounded.

At the beginning of the war, the Germans destroyed and sank twelve tankers, and damaged many refineries and cargo ships, paralyzing the waters of the Caribbean and the coast of South America.

Many merchant ships were also targeted; for instance, the father of Gary Sobers (the renowned cricketer) did not make it to England as his ship was targeted and sunk, taking him with it, along with many other West Indian men who had paid to board the ship in order to travel to Britain to join up and fight.

At this point, although thousands of miles away, the Caribbean became the front line for a time. In 1941, the Atlantic shipping lanes were important to the Germans with regard to disrupting traffic to the various theatres of war. Caribbean oil installations were also on their list of main targets, along with ports being infiltrated. Some ships were being sunk before they even had time to clear the port, as German U-boats were waiting just outside. This resulted in shortages of food, kerosene for cooking, and crude oil, as ships were being torpedoed by the submarines.

In 1942 the English Government at the time made it clear that they did not wish the men of the Caribbean to leave their country to fight. One of the reasons was because they did not want any disruption with the supply of raw materials they had been getting from their overseas territories. They were concerned that the decrease in manpower from the West Indies was to have an impact on Britain.

The army were also concerned about the idea of black soldiers killing whites, even though they were the enemy. They were concerned that it might degrade the idea of Empire.

They were still making it difficult for the Caribbean's to sign up, at one point, by demanding that they had to be of pure European descent to serve. As a black man, they were not valued enough to die for Britain at that time, although many did and have since, despite the many hoops that they had to jump through in order to join the services in Britain.

Due to the number of losses during the Battle of Britain in the RAF and other theatres of war, in the latter part of 1942, the government relented and black people were allowed to join the services. Indeed, there were two pilots who came from the West Indies and flew in the Battle of Britain.

The RAF had been forward-thinking and had already travelled to the West Indies in 1941 to look at recruiting pilots, navigators and ground crew. At the beginning, this was not done wholeheartedly due to their rules and regulations about it in the first place.

The BWIR (British West Indian Regiment) was formed, which comprised only of black men, with a white officer, as it was considered that only gentlemen could be officers. It was considered at that time that a black man could not be a gentleman. This Regiment was introduced with the blessing of King George VI, who stepped in and insisted that the formation go ahead as he could not afford to lose the war and his kingdom.

The Americans had now joined the war, after the events at Pearl Harbour on the 7th December 1941. Before then, they had held back. When they arrived in Britain, many of the servicemen began to cause problems between themselves and the black Caribbean servicemen who were already here.

There were fights, there was abuse and there was discrimination. This was because the American Army practised segregation, and could not understand how well the black Caribbean's appeared to be being treated, that they were allowed to go to whichever restaurant they wished and had the freedom of the towns.

They resented the fact that the black soldiers had the same rights and privileges as themselves. The hatred was so great that black Caribbean soldiers who had white wives were even beaten up and parted. At one point, the two sides were so busy fighting each other that it would appear this was more prevalent in their minds than the war.

Eventually, the American soldiers learned to leave the black British soldiers alone, as they began to realise that they were not subservient as their counterparts from America were. This was particularly as the British population began to dislike the way in which the Americans were treating the black soldiers, and when the Americans were on their way to the pubs, clubs, and restaurants, they were well warned.

At one point, many of the general British population said enough is enough and stood up to the Americans.

Some of the men from the British army would get involved in fights with the Americans if they were attacking the black British soldiers, as the general consensus was that they could insult their own black soldiers, however, they would not stand for foreigners from America doing so.

Recruiting in WWII

The RAF went to the West Indies and began their recruitment campaign in Trinidad, Jamaica, and Guiana, where they gave lectures to the men about the war effort. Tests were given to those who turned up. The men came from a myriad of backgrounds; some came from town, while others from poor rural areas. Only the very educated were chosen as pilots.

Trinidad & Tobago had a very high level of education, as did many of the English-speaking West Indian islands, where many secondary schools taught Latin; one specialised school in Trinidad taught Greek also. It was impossible to become a doctor or a lawyer in Trinidad unless you had Latin under your belt. To become a navigator or a pilot, one had to be that bit more educated. The aircrew was the cream of the crop, taken from each country.

In Trinidad, there was a Light Airplane Club not far from where the lectures were given, and so the recruited men chosen were taken there to have flying lessons. There were also navigation, maths, and metrological classes, as well as general planning and flying training.

On their arrival in England, they continued taking exams and received more training to become navigators and pilots, which, depending on their flying experience, could take anything from six months to two years.

Spitfires required one pilot, where Mosquitos were planes that required a two-man team, but being small, they did not need navigators, as their job was to shoot down enemy planes or take photographs on reconnaissance flights. However, the bombers, on the other hand, needed a navigator to find the target in order to bomb it. To that end, the bombers also used pathfinders that would fly over the location, drop a marker, and then fly straight up to get out of the way of the bombs before they hit the target, and for Caribbean pilots, this was the job they did.

Once in England and the training was completed, a seven-man crew was chosen for each plane and everyone would meet in a large room, pilots, navigators, gunners, and everyone that would be needed on a seven-man flight. The men were then allowed to speak to each other to see who would be most suited to work together.

It was said that the black aircrew would always be chosen as they were thought to be lucky, although they were not chosen as pilots in bombers, due to the Air Ministry's feeling that the other men would not take orders from them, as they would not trust their judgement.

This was a strange sentiment, since the navigators, (as many of the West Indian pilots became), were the ones who had to plot the route there and back while in the theatre of war. Without them, the bomber would be lost.

250 men volunteered from Trinidad to join the RAF, 50 of whom were killed within a short period of time after joining. The overall total loss was 55,000 aircrew in WWII, the majority being in Bomber Command.

Caribbean RAF Officers of WWII
Line-up includes:- front row, Dusty Miller, Orbett Liason, Ulric Cross, Johnny Smythe.
Third row ER Brathwaite

The Army was slightly different with regards to recruiting men for service. In the case of Barbados, an officer was sent over to the recruiting office in Bridgetown, lectures were given and an exam taken. However, speaking to veterans today, some feel that they were misled by what they were told in Barbados before they joined the service.

One soldier who was interviewed said that, while in Barbados in the recruiting office, they took a test and were told that they would not have to take another exam when they arrived in England, however, when they arrived, the impression was given that they could not take the test as they were not intelligent enough.

In his case, in particular, it did not make sense, as after his exam he was sent to join the Royal Hussars, which was a very prestigious regiment of the army. For some reason, the RAF did not seem to have as much trouble.

Flight L Arthur Weeks
Flight L Collins Joseph

Flight Lieutenant Arthur Weeks
Flight Sergeant Collins Joseph
Pilots on Spitfire

Flight L Arthur Weeks
Pilot

Flight Lieutenant Arthur Weeks was born in Barbados and was a Spitfire pilot with 132 (Bombay) Squadron. He can be seen on the cover of this book with Collins Joseph, who was also a Spitfire pilot.

Unfortunately, not a lot is known about Arthur Weeks, however, unlike Collins Joseph, he survived the war. Footage of Weeks shooting down an enemy plane can be seen on the Imperial War Museum website.

RAF Camera Gun Footage, Combat Film N0.73, Flight Officer Weeks 132 Squadron 21-12-1943, Spitfire 1x, Attacking FW 190

Pilot Officer Collins Joseph

Pilot Officer Collins Joseph was born in Trinidad and volunteered for the RAF in 1941, qualifying as a Spitfire pilot serving with N0. 130 Squadron. He died at the age of 28 years old while serving on a mission. There are different, conflicting versions as to how he died.

Some people claim that he went missing while flying from Liege to Aachen. It was believed that he may have been shot down by a Messerschmitt BF109. However, the Germans did not claim shooting down a Spitfire at the time he went missing.

Another theory is that he was killed by a "friendly fire" incident near Malmedy, in Belgium. It is even claimed that he may have died because his plane crashed due to mechanical failure.

What is known is that he was acquainted with Errol W. Barrow, who survived, and then entered politics, before serving as the Prime Minister of Barbados from 1966 – 1976.

Johnny Smythe OBE

Pilot Officer/Navigator, WWII. 1915-1996
Lancaster Bombers OBE- practising Barrister
Solicitor General for Republic of Sierra Leone

Johnny Smythe was born in Freetown, Sierra Leone in 1915 which is situated on the west coast of Africa.

Johnny Smythe is often mentioned when Caribbean navigators and pilots are discussed. This might be the case because they were an elite group, who moved in the same circles. He even ended up in the same POW camps as the Caribbean soldiers when he was captured by the Germans.

Johnny Smythe served with the Sierra Leone Defence Corps in 1939, reaching the rank of sergeant, before joining the RAF, and he did not arrive in Britain until 1940. One of his motivations was the refusal of Hitler to shake the hand of sportsman and medal winner, Jesse Owens in the 1936 Berlin Olympics, and the policies Hitler held about race.

As an RAF volunteer, he was a little bit ahead of when the powers that be decided that they would take on volunteers from the Caribbean. Hence why his first mission was in the RAF in 1941 when the majority of volunteers were taken on in 1942.

Smythe was promoted to Flying Officer. However, on the night of 18th November 1943, he was shot down on his 28th mission.

He said, "As the bullets rained on us, we were flying at 16,000 ft when the fighters came out of nowhere. They raked the fuselage and there were flames everywhere. Then the searchlights caught us. I was hit by shrapnel. Pieces came from underneath, piercing my abdomen, going through my side. Another came through my seat and into my groin. I heard the pilot ordering us to bail out. We had some rough ones before but this seemed to be the end." Johnny was able to parachute to the ground at which point he hid in a barn.

He continues, "Men in uniform came into the barn where I was hiding behind some straw. Then they opened up, raking the place with automatic fire. I decided to give in. The Germans couldn't believe their eyes. I'm sure that's what saved me from being shot immediately. To see a black man – and an officer at that – was more than they could come to terms with. They just stood there gazing."

Smythe spent eighteen months in Pomerania, Germany, in a prison camp for officers in Stalag Luft1. While imprisoned there, he helped others escape, but could not himself, (as in the case of Cy Grant), since he was 6'1" and black, and would not blend into the population very well in Germany. However, he was rescued by the Russians in 1945, who hugged him and gave him vodka on their arrival.

Smythe returned home after the war and worked in the Colonial Office. However, he decided to return to England in 1948. He had returned on the ship "Empire Windrush", which had been a captured German ship. It brought 500 West Indian ex-servicemen and workers, and other nationalities to the UK.

After studying Law in 1950 and passing his law exams, he then married his fiancée from Grenada in 1951 and sailed back to Freetown.

Johnny Smythe became Solicitor General of Sierra Leone in 1961, after which, in 1963, he went on a lecture tour of the eastern United States.

In 1978, Johnny Smythe received an OBE – (Order of the British Empire) and moved back to England in 1993 with his wife and 5 children. He died in 1996 in Thame, Oxfordshire.

James Hyde

Flight Sergeant James Hyde
Spitfire Pilot

Flight Sergeant James Hyde of San Juan, Trinidad, was a Spitfire pilot who arrived in Britain in 1942. After training and qualifying with the RAF, he flew with 132 Squadron, where he met Errol Barrow who became Prime Minister of Barbados. He was also featured in a film produced by the BBC, (which also included Ulric Cross) about WWII service personnel.

James was pictured in 1944 with his Squadron's mascot, a dog called 'Dingo', who was the squadron commander's pet dog, at Detling, Kent, England. James is wearing a life jacket, known universally as a Mae West, and is holding an oxygen mask and his flying gloves. Most air battles took place at altitudes in excess of 15,000 feet and oxygen and thermal protection were vital.

Flight Sergeant James Hyde was providing aerial cover during the battle of Arnhem when he was killed after a dog fight and being shot down in combat by a Messerschmitt and crashed in Elst near Nijmegen, Holland. He was 27 years old at the time.

The normal duration for a pilot in WWII was 25 - 30 flights; if you made it to that, you were out and your job was done. Many pilots did more, if they lived, however, most did not survive.

He was buried in Jonkerbos military cemetery. His parents were Joseph and Millicent Hyde, of San Juan, Trinidad.

E.R. Brathwaite

RAF Fighter Pilot WWII
Writer, Diplomat
1912-2016
Known for the book "To Sir with Love"

Eustace Edward Ricardo Brathwaite was born in Georgetown, British Guiana (now Guyana) on the 27th of June 1912. After living in Britain, he moved to the U.S. and lived in Washington D.C. However, when he passed away, he was living in Rockville, Maryland, U.S.A.

He came from a privileged background as both his parents went to Oxford University, which meant that he grew up in an environment that involved education, achievement parental guidance and pride. Brathwaite attended Queen's College, Guyana, and later The City College of New York.

E.R Brathwaite once said, "When I decided to move to England it was in pursuit of education. I was determined that I was not going to let any one or group of persons interfere with that".

Not much is known about ER Brathwaite's RAF years. One can only surmise, like most men of colour in the service, not much notice was taken of him. However, we know that he did participate in WWII by joining the RAF and becoming a fighter pilot. He would later describe his experience in the RAF as, "I did not feel discriminated against because of my skin colour or ethnicity, I was just another pilot".

After the war, he studied at Cambridge, leaving with a master's degree in physics in 1949. After not being able to find work, he became disillusioned. Due to a chance meeting with an acquaintance, he decided to become a teacher, while having his eye on something else.

Brathwaite wrote the book "To Sir with Love" about the time he spent teaching in an East End school. He said, "I was given a card by the children I was teaching, and on it was written, "To Sir with Love". It was at this point I started to enjoy being a black teacher, being me".

However, despite the book becoming a hit, and having a film made of it starring Sidney Poitier, he disliked the film, as he felt that it was too sentimental, and did not include somethings as they were.He was a high achiever; later in life, he became the Human Rights officer for the World Veterans' Federation and later a consultant for UNESCO, and in 1966 was appointed

Guyana's representative to the United Nations. He then became Guyana's ambassador to Venezuela and taught at various American universities. (At one point, he was on the Board of Trustees for the Krasnow Institute of George Mason University).

He went on to write many books. They were banned in South Africa. However, while on a six-week trip to South Africa in 1973, the ban on his books was lifted, and he was granted the title of "honorary white", which he detested.

When ER Braithwaite died, he was 104 years old. He had been many things, but most of all, as a pilot, he fought for a country that he felt was worth fighting for.

Larry Osbourne OBE

Larry Osbourne OBE
Wing Commander
December 1922 - March 1996
Joined RAF 1943
Navigator

Group Captain Larry Osbourne, OBE, had a varied career in the RAF, from navigator and Air Traffic Controller to supply specialist. He came from a modest upbringing in Trinidad and became a high-ranking officer in the RAF, who initially did his training in Canada.

In 1942, while in Trinidad, Larry Osbourne met some pilots from the 53 Squadron Coastal Command who were stationed at the Waller Field Air Base. He immediately became fascinated by aviation and with the planes and the men who flew them. He arrived in England in 1943 and had no hesitation in volunteering for the Royal Air Force (RAF). He was trained as a navigator and was posted to the Coastal Command Catalina Squadron, doing anti-submarine patrols over the Atlantic.

After the war, he switched branches and became an RAF air traffic controller in the fast-developing world of radar interception by jet aircraft. As a Wing Commander, he was appointed to the Anglo-German Commission charged with overseeing the rebirth and development of the new German Luftwaffe for NATO. His final job with the RAF was the introduction of computers in all their various forms and functions into the service. He retired as an Air Commodore in 1977 with an OBE.

Larry Osbourne was a man of many talents, who spoke German and Welsh.

He was reported as saying:

> "If people retain their prejudices after knowing me for a short while, it's probably my fault for failing to impress my personality on them." Colour was never an issue for him in the RAF and with people who knew him.

> "Group Captain Larry Osbourne, OBE, born December 27th, 1922. Navigator, air traffic controller, and supply specialist, died in the month of March at the age of seventy-three".

Errol Barrow PC, QC

Flying Officer Errol Barrow, PC, QC
21 January 1920 - 1st June 1987
WW11 Pilot
First Prime Minister of Barbados
Attorney at Law

Errol Barrow was born in the parish of St Lucy, Barbados and was the son of Rev. Reginald Grant Barrow and Ruth Barrow.

His parents were political activists and, as a boy, he was determined to fight for civil rights and social justice. A gifted student, Errol Barrow won three scholarships, the last in 1939 to study Classics at Codrington College. With the outbreak of war, however, the young Barbadian travelled to Britain to volunteer for the RAF.

Errol Barrow enlisted in the RAF on the 31st December 1940 and flew 45 operational bombing missions over the European theatre. He was posted to 88 Squadron, completing 45 bombing operations against targets in occupied Europe.Leader Alfred Barnes remembered him as: "A bloody good navigator-first class. Get you there, get you back. Can't ask more than that can you, eh? Never saw Barrow get in a flap. A good man to have along."

By 1945, he had risen to the rank of Flying Officer and was appointed as personal navigator to the Commander in Chief of the British Zone of occupied Germany in WWII. After his studies, Barrow returned to Barbados to practice as a barrister.

In 1955, he formed the Democratic Labour Party (DLP) to press for rapid social and political reform and independence from British rule. The DLP came to power in 1961. Barrow served as Premiere, leading his country to independence on 30th November 1966.

As Prime Minister of Barbados, Barrow enacted a series of measures aimed at reducing poverty and ignorance and improving the quality of life of ordinary Barbadians. These included educational, health and nutritional reforms, the introduction of National Insurance, and the provision of social services for all. He also did much to develop industry, commerce, and tourism on the island.

Barrow was dedicated to lessening Barbados' economic and political reliance on foreign powers, especially the United States. He was, in addition, a champion of strengthening the ties between the English-speaking countries of the Caribbean.

Errol Barrow served as Prime Minister until 1976. He returned to power with an overwhelming majority in May 1986 but died in office on 1st July 1987, aged only 67.

2020 heralds 100 years since Errol Burrow was born. Celebrations were held all over the Island, and on the 21st of January 2020, an open day was arranged to celebrate his 100th birthday. An advertisement was placed in the local newspaper by the Barbados Light Aeroplane Club, detailing the different events that were going to take place on the day.

Phillip Louis Ulric Cross DSO DFO

Squadron Leader Philip Louie Ulric Cross

Enlisted 1941; Bomber Command; 8 Group; Pathfinder
80 missions; awarded DSO (Distinguished Service Order)
and DFC (Distinguished Flying Cross) in1944; presented
with 12 decorations while serving in the 2nd World War.
He received his Medal of Honour from King George.
After the war, he became a High Court Judge, and
The High Commissioner for Trinidad and Tobago.
Born - Trinidad 1-05-1917 - 2014

Ulric Cross was born in Trinidad in 1917. He was highly intelligent, very articulate and fluent in both Greek and Latin, which was a requirement for holding a professional job like a lawyer or doctor in Trinidad.

An Interview with Ulric Cross

The first time I met Ulric Cross was at his brother's home for a scheduled interview. He led me into a large sunny room where there stood a very tall (6' at least), well-dressed, impressive-looking character; from his well-groomed hair and pressed suit, down to his shiny shoes, he was well presented.

After shaking my hand, he motioned me to sit down, smiled and asked "How are you?", immediately putting me at ease. I was taken by his presence and how, at 90 years old plus, not only was he tall and distinguished-looking, but also how well-spoken he was. There was a constant twinkle in his eye, that told you that life was for living, a smile and laughter that embodied fun, and an ease about him that made you feel relaxed, as if he was speaking to his best friend.

I asked Ulric what people did between WWI and WWII he said, "Between the wars in Trinidad, the young men played cricket in the dry season, football in the rainy season, and you read all seasons. We had no television and no radio, that's why we read. We were more academic and they taught Latin in every school. This was normal. Fortunately, I also learned Greek in mine. Standards were high. Today, Trinidadians do not read. This is because of the television."

Ulric had belonged to a book club, which had also joined the International Book Club, and so the group read everything they could get their hands on, including

Hitler's Mein Kampf, so he was well versed in what was going on in the world.

Ulric said, "Britain stood alone. Hitler had conquered most of Europe, and the world was drowning in fascism".

America was not yet in the war, so he decided to do something about it and volunteered to fight in the RAF, along with several members of his book club, because as he said, "They all wanted to be pilots".

A representative from the RAF was sent to Trinidad on a recruiting drive. Luckily, there was a small flying school nearby. This made it possible to give flying training there while giving lectures.

Ulric's training also included exams which included a physical, and this was of some concern to him, so he decided to prepare for it and went on a diet of milk and bananas. "Why?" I asked. He replied, "Because milk was considered the perfect food, (because it is 1/3 carbohydrate, 1/3 protein, 1/3 fat) and bananas were hermetically sealed".

This interview was not the last time that I met Ulric Cross. We planned a trip to the Cameroon Embassy in Holland Park, London on the 5th April 2011, to collect a certificate which was awarded to him sometime before.

When I think of him today, I remember after coming out of the Cameroon Embassy, I told him that if he waited at the entrance outside, I would go and call him a taxi in order to get him home. As I was about to turn away, he took out a cigarette and lit it up. "Ulric!" I cried "Don't do that! Those things will kill you!" He stopped and looked at me, threw his head back and gave out a hearty laugh. It stopped me in my tracks.

What was I thinking? This is a man that went on 80 missions under fire over Germany, was shot down seven times, and survived! As I walked away, I glanced back at him and said, "As you were". We both laughed.

The last time I saw him was not long before he died, when he asked me to go to Trinidad to see him on his birthday and join the celebrations. There, his daughter Nicole and I laughed at the fact that I was so in awe of her father.

Leaving Trinidad for Britain

Ulric left Trinidad for Britain at the age of 24 years old in 1941. On his arrival, there was more training, at which he excelled. He was not only trained as a navigator/pilot, but as a wireless operator, and had skills in bomb aiming, and Morse code. He also excelled in Maths.

Once in operation, he flew 80 sorties, non-stop operations over Germany and is respected by everyone who knew him. This feat was marvellous in itself, as most people did 25-30 missions and stopped, or got shot down and didn't make it. However, Ulric said, "I had to keep going because I knew that if I had stopped, I would not be able to get back into a plane again".

Ulric Cross was shot down 7 times, one of which was as he flew over Germany as a navigator with the pilot whose name was Jack.

On one occasion, they were in a Mosquito bomber flying through heavy flak, and Jack was pulling Ulric's leg by asking how he ended up with a German name like Ulric. His reply was that he would ask about it when he got home. "If we get home," Jack said. "Don't worry, "Ulric said, "we will get home; I'm the navigator, I'll get us home".

Just as they lined up for the bombing run, the plane rocked violently, then as they released the bombs on target, the whistles of their falling bombs changed to a horrific exploding sound. They could see the flak and tracers going past them. Boom! The plane rocked violently again with impact, careering off its ascent, now locked into a deadly descent.

With the right engine on fire, Ulric and Jack sprang into action. "Jack! pull up, pull up!" Ulric shouted, "I am! I am! If I pulled any harder, I'd rip out the stick!" Jack shouted back, over the noise of the descending plane. Finally, they were able to level out, and Ulric plotted a new course for home, as they could not make the previous one due to lack of fuel and the engine being on fire, while losing height rapidly.

With the base at Swanton Morley in sight, they could see from the angle that the plane was going to run out of runway. It was also pitch black and they could not radio the base to tell them that they were in trouble and coming in. The crew weighed up their odds. "Right then, Ulric. We're going in," Jack said. "Blast" was the word used as they passed the mark on the runway, confirming that they were going to overshoot.

Even at this point, jokes were made - "There wouldn't be a pillow factory behind those hedges, would there?" A moment later they hit the quarry. Then silence.

Ulric and Jack were able to walk away from the plane. The first sound was Jack's voice, "That was a close one and I have a smashing headache to prove it! But well done getting us home, Ulric!" "Thanks, Jack for your magnificent flying! My head hurts like the Dickens but at least it lets me know I'm alive."

The near-death experience prompted Squadron Leader Ulric Cross to reflect on his life, and he went on to do great work, and live life to the full.

The Caribbean navigators and pilots knew or had heard of each other as there was a small enough amount of them, in the beginning, to do so.

Ulric Cross met Cy Grant after the war. He had also been shot down but had spent years in the Stalag Luft POW prison camp of the 'Great Escape' fame.

In Ulric's words, "they became fast friends". They decided to take up Law together and were eventually called to the bar at Middle Temple in London. On leaving the exam room after finishing the last exam, they looked at each other and Ulric said, "Never for the rest of my life, will I ever do another exam." Cy replied, "Me too," and with that, they left and went to see what Ulric described as the most "stupid film they could find called Lust in the Dust". Ulric said, "Cy was extremely good-looking and I believe that the aristocratic women of the day called him 'The Debs' Delight.' I wasn't so lucky," he said.

Ulric Cross had an illustrious career. He was called to the bar in 1949. He later became a producer for BBC Radio. It was at this point that he left the U.K to go to Africa. He spent two years in Ghana, then between 1960 and 1961 he was Senior Crown Counsel, then Attorney General in Cameroon and then, in 1967, he became a High Court Judge in Tanzania.

After a number of high-powered legal positions, including Professor of Law in Tanzania, Ulric Cross returned to Trinidad and went from being a High Court Judge to High Commissioner for Trinidad and Tobago.

I remember thinking, what a great role model for young men, not only of colour, as he showed resilience, courage, and determination in his life, which meant that nothing was impossible once you put your mind to it and worked at it.

HIGH COMMISSION FOR THE REPUBLIC OF CAMEROON
Peace-Work-Fatherland

HAUT COMMISSARIAT POUR LA REPUBLIQUE DU CAMEROUN
Paix-Travail-Patrie

REQUEST FOR INTERVIEW
DEMANDE D'AUDIENCE

Person requested / Personne demandée: HIGH COMMISSIONER

Name of visitor / Nom du visiteur: P. L. U. CROSS

Rank / Qualité: FORMER ATTORNEY GENERAL

Object of interview / Objet de la demande: RECEIPT OF CHEVALIER OF ORDER OF VALOUR

London, / Londres: 5 April 2011

Signature:

Written by Ulric on the day he and I visited the Cameroon High Commission to collect his certificate and medal.

At the Cameroon Embassy where Ulric is holding the certificate which he and I went to collect.

Men of Valour

Left to right

Flight Officer Dudley Thomson, Jamaica;
Flight Lieutenant Osmund Kelsick, D.F.C Montserrat;
Flight Officer Ronald Hall, British Guiana;
Flight Lieutenant (Squadron Leader) Ulric Cross, D.S.O., D.F.C., Trinidad

These men all played a vital part in the war, some as navigators others as pilots. All, however, were trained to fly.

This was a gathering for a radio show on the BBC, highlighting the RAF. Few would have realised or given it a thought that they were black pilots, two of whom had flown in the Battle of Britain against the Germans.

CY Grant – Navigator/Pilot - Prisoner of war

Cy Grant Enlisted: - RAF 1941 — 103, Squadron (Bomber Command) Lancaster Bomber. Shot down 1943 – Became prisoner of Nazis - 2 years in Stalag Luft 111 Prisoner of War camp in Silesia made famous in the film "The Great Escape".

Flight Lieutenant, Barrister, BBC Presenter, Actor, Writer

Born British Guiana (South America) now Guyana.
8th November 1919 - 2010

Cy had an extraordinary life. Not only did he have a distinguished war record winning several medals, but when he left the RAF, he reinvented himself several times. He was called to the bar with Ulric Cross, his friend, to become a barrister, although he could not practise his trade because of his colour.

In the years that followed, he became a successful writer, BBC presenter, and a film star working with the likes of Richard Burton and Joan Collins, to mention a few. He also started up many organisations, which have enriched the Arts for the black community, using his knowledge from working with Sir Lawrence Olivier.

He was born on the 8th of November 1919 in the village of Beterverwagting, in what was then known as British Guiana, South America into an upper-middle-class family.

His mother was considered to be a great beauty. Her father had been a Scotsman, and a sergeant in charge of prisons near English Harbour. She became a school teacher, who taught piano in a British school. His father was a respected and proud black prominent Moravian priest with a large church and congregation. One of seven children, the family moved to New Amsterdam, Berbice (in Guyana) when he was 11 years old. His father had a great influence on him and taught him about Alexandre Dumas and others such as Alexander Pushkin, who had black ancestors and were great leaders.

Guyana had conformed to colonial attitudes and judged its population by the darkness of their skin- the lighter your skin, the more valued you were in society. Those that met Cy Grant described him as a good-looking, knowledgeable man, all of 6'2", of mixed race, with a commanding presence. With these attributes, Cy found himself with more advantages and privileges than most people of colour. It was not until after the war, he said, and living in England, that he realised that he was black, as he had never thought of himself as such.

Cy Grant's Family: Father, Sisters, Mother, Brother, Sister, Cy Grant

During the war, he was assigned to 103 Squadron of Bomber Command based at Elsham Wolds, Lincolnshire. One of his colleagues was Don Towers, an English airman who manned the radio on the bomber, and one of the seven crew members who was shot down with him over the Ruhr valley. Cy was the Lancaster's navigator on the night in 1943 over Holland, when, while returning from a bombing mission over the Ruhr, they were shot down. Cy said, "Suddenly, Jo Addison shouted over the intercom that a German fighter was closing in from underneath us. Addison then opened fire on it, and moments later it was in Geoffrey Wallis' sights, so he immediately opened fire also. In a second, it seemed, it had disappeared".

However, after a minute or two of calm, and they were on their way home, they realised that they were on fire. Alton, the pilot, put the plane into a dive to put the fire out and then levelled out. For a moment all was calm again, then they realised that it was worse than they thought; they had been hit.

Soon after, one of the undercarriage wheels fell away in a flaming circle. (They did not know then but it fell on a farmhouse and killed the farmer's wife outright.) They knew at that point that they were not going to be able to cross the Channel and get back home, so they changed course and headed back inland.

As the plane disintegrated around them, there was nothing the men could do but jump and hope their parachutes opened and that they were not on fire. As they began to pile up at the escape hatch, the decision to jump was taken away from them as the plane exploded. Five men out of the seven survived the crash. The engineer, Ron Hollywood and the tail-gunner, Joseph Addison were killed.

Cy landed in a field away from his crew, where he had to spend the night hiding in fear of attracting attention. Eventually, he was found by a young boy Joost, Klootwijk aged 14 years, who ran back to tell his father what he had discovered. Eventually, he was given over to the Dutch police, who sent a man to collect him on a motorbike. Escaping did cross his mind, however, a black RAF serviceman in uniform making his way across the land would have drawn too much attention.

So, he ignored the gun protruding out of the policeman's holster and went easily as he was handed over to the Gestapo. After paying a visit to the farmer and his son and threatening them, without much joy, the Gestapo packed him off to Stalag Luft 111, where he was reunited with his radio operator, Don Towers.

Don Towers

When I met Don Towers, I wasn't too surprised at how tall he was. He was at least 6'2" tall. I noted that all of the RAF aircrew I met were very tall. He was in his 90s and had a good recollection of what had gone on during the last flight that the crew made over the Ruhr valley.

I asked him how he came to be one of the crew on Cy's Lancaster.

He said that "at the end of their training, he and some others were invited to a coffee morning. They were men who had all the different principles needed to man a Lancaster plane; each man had a specialised role. In the room were pilots, navigators, bomb-aimers, wireless operators, flight engineers, mid-gunners, and rear-gunners.

At some point, they would have to form a crew; for instance, a pilot might speak to four or five navigators to see which one he could get along with. At the end of the day, he would choose six men to join him to form a seven-man crew. Black navigators were very popular as they were considered lucky. The pilot would also have the knowledge that his navigator was able to fly a plane, which could only have been a bonus."

Don explained that although there were procedures as to how or who left the plane first if they had to abandon it, as it was on fire, everyone was getting backed up at the exit hatch. This was inevitable as it was known that the escape hatch on the Lancaster bomber, only 2' x 2', was far too small for a quick getaway or an exit of a full complement of men. Having a parachute strapped to your back did not make it any easier.

The Air Ministry was aware of the problem but did nothing at the time. It was later noted that it was felt that if the front hatch was bigger, the aircrew would be tempted to abandon the aircraft prematurely, instead of sticking it out and returning to base.

However, in this case, the fact that the exit hatch was too small was academic as the plane exploded, sending the men flying into the air. Although he survived, the pilot, unfortunately, broke his neck and was left after the war holding his head at a strange angle.

While in the POW camp, before they were moved, Don was aware through the camp grapevine that Cy was in the same camp, but did not see him as he was in a different part of the prison. He knew, however, that Cy had become an entertainer as he played guitar and piano and could sing.

To this end, he entertained the German soldiers as a diversion while the other men dug the tunnels, named 'Tom', 'Dick', and 'Harry', which were eventually to become part of the Great Escape, the mass escape which was later made into a film of the same name. He helped his fellow prisoners with their escape plans even though he knew that he could not escape himself, due to being a man of colour. He knew he would not be able to melt into the population if he had escaped, which was the reason he did not escape when he was first captured.

Don returned home from the war with a special diary in hand. While Don was in the POW camp, he kept a diary of sketches in which other inmates were allowed to write and draw.

I felt fortunate to have met someone that was actually on the flight and that had survived the POW camp of the Great Escape. Unfortunately, a year after I had interviewed him, Don passed away. As I had also been to his wife's funeral some time before, it seemed to be the end of an era.

Don Towers – Book from POW Camp

After the war, he studied law as a barrister and was called to the bar at Middle Temple, London. However, due to his colour, he was unable to practise. No legal firms would offer him a pupillage course, something that is still happening even in 2020.

In the end, Cy became disillusioned with a society that would allow you to fight for King and Country but, in his own words, he was "not welcome to seek a seat at the high table of the military establishment. No Othello's allowed".

Cy then worked for the BBC and became the first black man to appear regularly on the BBC. Most of us, who were children or adults around that time, would remember him as the person who sang regular Calypso songs about current affairs on the "Tonight" programme, with Cliff Mitchelmore in 1957. In later years, he described how he saw himself as a typecast, one-dimensional troubadour.

Cy Grant also appeared as the voice of Captain Green in the children's programme, 'Captain Scarlet'.

He also appeared in films, one of which was alongside Richard Burton and Joan Collins, called "Sea Wife", which caused controversy as some of the actors did not want him to be portrayed as the hero, although that was the role at the start of the film. 'Shaft in Africa', was another film he appeared in, and many more, along with a film about Bomber Command in 1943 for the BBC with Dirk Bogarde. This was a propaganda film showing that there were black aircrew in the RAF.

As a singer, he was able to make records, one of which was The Lord's Prayer, sold through Parlophone Records.

Cy auditioned for Laurence Olivier and appeared in London's West End as well as in New York in 1965. Later, he played Othello at the Phoenix Theatre, Leicester, and was the first man of colour to do so since Paul Robeson.

Cy Grant died at the age of 90 in 2010. Sadly, he died before black servicemen could march at the Cenotaph as an entity. On Remembrance Day, he would stand in the crowd as the military passed by, holding his medals in his pocket. A sad footnote for a man of great talent and knowledge.

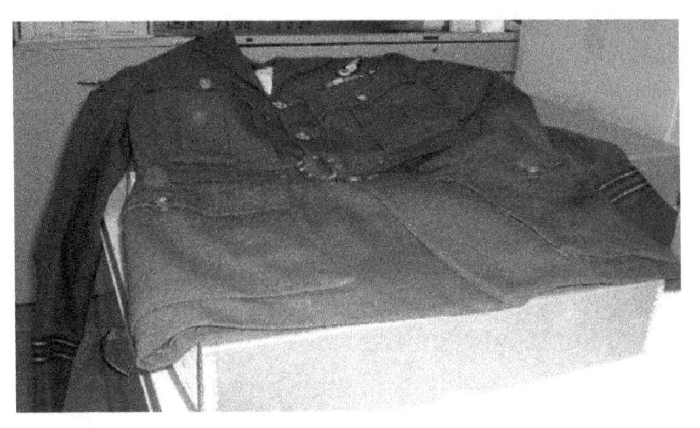

Cy Grants Jacket

Cy Grants Crew consist of: -
103 Squadron

Pilot:	Flying Officer Alton Langille (Canada)
Navigator:	Pilot Officer Cy Grant (British Guyana)

Wireless Operator:	Pilot Office Don Towers (England)
Bomb aimer:	Pilot Officer Charles Reynolds (England)
Flight engineer:	Sergeant Ronald Hollywood (England)
Air Gunner:	Geoffrey Wallis (England)
Air gunner:	Pilot Officer Joseph Addison (Canada)

Lest we forget

Basil Anderson

Basil Anderson was an air gunner of 218 Squadron, Lancaster bomber.

On the 23rd of October 1943, his plane was attacked by German fighters. With his aircraft crippled and on fire, all the crew bailed out and joined what was called the Caterpillar Club. This was a name given to men who had successfully used a parachute to get out of a disabled aircraft. The fact that the parachutes were made out of silk gave kudos to the name also.

Anderson evaded immediate capture and walked for one week before the Germans caught up with him. He was made a prisoner of war and sent to Stalag Luft 4B. Determined not to remain in the camp, he carried out a daring escape and managed to reach the river Elbe, but being unable to cross, he was caught and returned to the same camp where he was put into the solitary cells for three months.

He had not completed his time in solitary when he did the impossible and escaped from the solitary confinement cells into the main prison camp. He was hidden in the main camp while a frantic search was carried out for him by the Germans. As soon as ID and suitable clothes were acquired for him, he walked out of Stalag Luft 4B disguised as a French Army POW.

The Germans captured him for the second time and he was put back in prison. However, he was transferred to Stalag Luft 111 where he met other Trinidadians, Arnold Kelshaw and Gareth Lindia.

Not too long afterwards, the Russians took over the camp and they kept the RAF prisoners locked up. Once again, Anderson escaped, this time from the Russians by stealing a bicycle and pedalling furiously away.

A few days later he was knocked down by a Russian army truck driver; the drunk Cossack never bothered to stop. With a broken leg, Anderson continued until, astonishingly, he found a German family who would hide him from the Russians.

Eventually, the Russians recaptured him and set his broken leg in one of their field hospitals. In time, he was handed over to the Allies, however, while in a US hospital in Rheims, it was discovered that five bones in his leg had been badly set. This meant that he had to have surgery to correct the problem. It was sometime before he could leave the RAF. He should be remembered for his courage, as he was a truly daring adventurer and son of Trinidad.

Sam King

Sam Beaver King MBE
RAF Ground Crew
20th February 1926 – 17th June 2016
First Black Mayor of Southwark

Sam King was one of ten children and lived with his parents in Jamaica on their banana farm. He decided to join the Royal Air Force in 1944, after reading a newspaper article in Jamaica, calling for volunteers.

He underwent some training in Kingston before travelling to England, first to Filey in Yorkshire, then on to RAF Hawkinge, (a fighter base near Folkestone in Kent), where he worked as an engineer.

As ground crew in the RAF, he repaired planes after they came back from the theatre of war. He had a good relationship with the pilots as they knew that it was only due to good work by him and others like him, (who were repairing the planes) that they were able to return safely to the base. He inspired confidence in his professionalism because he spoke with knowledge and conviction.

After the war and being demobilised in 1947, he returned to Jamaica. However, he found that he could not find work or settle, so he returned to England on the 'Empire Windrush'.

I asked him several questions, one of which was if he thought that young men should join the forces today. He felt very strongly about the question and said, "I think that young men should be called upon for national service, as it is a good thing for them to gain discipline, and increase the strength of character. Furthermore, I think that if someone had committed two offences against society, they should be sent to do one year to eighteen months of national service, as a given".

On his return to England on the 'Windrush', Sam King soon became a prominent campaigner for the West Indies community, and along with Arthur Torrington, set up The Windrush Foundation, a charitable organisation dedicated to keeping alive the memories of the young men and women who fought for Britain.

He also had a hand in setting up the Carnival in St Pancras Town Hall with Claudia Jones, which in turn became the precursor for the Notting Hill Carnival.

He served as a local councillor for six months before being elected as mayor of the London Borough of Southwark in 1993. He became known as "Mr Windrush" after campaigning to establish a public holiday to mark the contributions of immigrants to British society.

Sam King said that "We must contribute everything from the House of Lords to the schoolroom; we are proud of the fabric of this country and we should contribute where we can".

As part of "Windrush Day", King was appointed an MBE in 1998. He also wrote a book called "Climbing up the Rough Side of the Mountain".

Sadly, Sam King passed away on the 17th of June 2017, at 90 years old. He had two children and was married twice.

Jeremy Corbyn said at his funeral, "He educated Londoners with Caribbean food, Caribbean culture, Caribbean music. London is a better place, and Britain is a better place thanks to him".

Alexander Fraser

Flying Officer Pilot

Alexander Fraser was a pilot trainee with the 5th ETS Course at Piarco before moving on to advanced training in England.

After qualifying as a fighter pilot, he was posted to 268 Squadron, where he flew a Mustang AFD 559 fighter plane.

On 27th May 1944, he was flying in formation in a Mustang AFD 559, when at 15.40hrs, south of Gatwick Airport, when another Mustang, whose pilot was disoriented, collided with him. He was 21 years old.

The tail was cut completely off Fraser's aircraft by the propeller of the Mustang and he was killed in the resulting crash. The tragic accident cut short what might have been a promising career, but from a statistical point of view, he was the only pilot from Trinidad and Tobago who lost his life while flying the Mustang.

His parents were Dickson and Annie C. Fraser of Port of Spain, Trinidad. Fraser was buried in Forfar Cemetery, Angus, Scotland.

Women in Service

In general, the women of WWII were looked on as a group who took on jobs that men would have normally done in order to free up the men to fight for their country. Within the various groups of women from different countries, there were exceptions.

Russian women, for instance, were looked at in a different way and were seen as being as capable as the men. This was partly due to the communist revolution in 1917 when the population was seen as being equal. For instance, there were women who volunteered as pilots, many of whom had learned to fly in youth organizations, which meant that, by the end of the war, more than one in ten Soviet combat pilots were women.

However, the experiences of the Caribbean women and the English women were completely different. Caribbean women were not given the chance to show how capable they were, and so were given what they considered to be more menial jobs. For example, they were allowed to work as nurses (however, at first only to Caribbean men), along with administration work.

Meanwhile, the experience of the English girls was completely different. The Queen was used as an example as she joined the Land Army, so there was already an expectation of their capabilities.

They were allowed to ferry planes all over Britain in readiness for the pilots to reach their destinations abroad easier. They did other jobs such as adjutant drivers, working in the operating rooms, secretaries, and land girls, while being showered with admiration and praise. Their efforts were celebrated individually and collectively.

The respective government offices at the time reluctantly decided to allow Caribbean women to join the forces. However, when they felt that they had to, restrictions were put in place, that would only affect the black Caribbean women, but not the white.

The Government decided to only permit black, middle-class women, of good character and family, who were well-mannered, preferably light-skinned, well-educated and financially viable (who would be in a position to pay their own fare from the West Indies to travel to England) to join the Services. Meanwhile, the white Caribbean women were welcomed, whatever their class, education level or financial viability. They were accepted without question and were not vetted; their ticket was their colour.

Having had a privileged upbringing, these middle-class, black Caribbean women were shocked (some even wept) at the conditions they were made to endure while travelling by sea to England. For example, some had to use dirty sugar bags on the floor as beds. However, when they did join the services, they found that, out of all of the armed services, they received the best treatment in the RAF.

Sacrifices were made; for instance, the general consensus in the Caribbean at the time of World War 11 was that young women should not leave home unless they were married. Therefore, for those parents who allowed their girls to travel to England on their own, it was a great sacrifice, and for some families who could not travel with them, it was a sacrifice that they were not prepared to make.

After the war, some young women did go back to the West Indies as the consensus was that it was better to be something in their own country than nothing in another.

The white Caribbean women who joined the ATS were sent to Washington, as the Americans would not accept the black Caribbean women, so they were sent to Scotland instead.

The women found that they were facing the same glass ceiling that was also in place against the black fighting men of the Caribbean. In the government's minds, they would only be given jobs that were considered to be minor, almost as a token. This led to them experiencing discrimination from the public and in some instances, from their superior officers. There was a story of one of the girls requesting a pair of shoes, who was told by the officer in charge, that she did not need any as she didn't use them where she came from.

ATS

It is possible that the reason why they did not receive the recognition they deserved, was because they were treated as one homogenous group and very little effort was made to recognise individual presence and achievement unless it was so extraordinary that it could not be ignored. Therefore, they were not acknowledged properly in history. To date, there is little that could be found in print about their work achievements, and even fewer photographs of them.

Yet still, the Caribbean women worked hard, and in a professional manner, doing the job that they were trained for, and for a time in Britain, were acknowledged as the best in their field.

When speaking to them today, one gets a sense that they are proud that they were able to serve the nation, and even more proud of the good work they felt that they were able to undertake, even with the difficulties they were faced with.

Joyce Cyrus

Joyce Cyrus

Joyce Cyrus from Trinidad and Tobago was the first woman from Trinidad to become a WAAF (Women's Auxiliary Air Force) in World War Two. She was attached to 139 Pathfinder Squadron for general duties.

The Women's Auxiliary Air Force, also known as the WAAFs, was part of the RAF and was established in 1939. By 1943 its number was over 180,000.

Conscription of women began in 1914 and only for women between 20 and 30 years old. They were given basic training at one of five sites, after which point, they had a choice of the auxiliary services or factory work.

Conscription, however, did not apply to the Caribbean. They joined as volunteers.

They had a variety of roles, including compiling weather reports, maintaining aircraft, servicing on airfields, packing parachutes, the crewing of barrage balloons, radar, analysing reconnaissance photographs and working in intelligence. However, they did not serve as aircrew, as the women pilots were limited to the Air Transport Auxiliary (ATA), which was civilian. However, as a Caribbean woman, she was exempt from many of these duties.The WAAF women were exposed to the same dangers, as many worked at military installations.

On the 1st February 1949, they were renamed the Women's Royal Air Force.

Caribbean Woman at War

The 6888 Battalion

Reviewing the troops in England,
Major Charity Adams (front, right) and Capt. Abbie Campbell inspect Woman's Army Corps members assigned to overseas duty during WWII

The 6888 Battalion

The Central Post of Directory Battalion was also known as the 6888 Battalion. They were a black battalion of American women who were seconded to England to run the mail service for the men fighting abroad. This was necessary as the British and the French incurred a huge backlog of mail destined for the battlefield, which they were unable to shift.

The department which represented the Battalion put forward the motion for them to take up the role abroad of sorting out the backlog of mail.

The Battalion was created by seconding 31 black women officers from the WAC, Army Service Force and the Army Air Force to create the one Battalion, thus creating the 6888 Battalion as it was known.

As troops moved at pace into Germany in 1945, there was a recognition that one of the most important things to ensure success was to maintain soldier morale and receiving letters from home would give a very necessary boost to those in service.

Mail was piling up in aeroplane hangars undelivered, particularly at Christmas, when the backlog was massive.

There were seven million Americans in Europe with similar names to the Europeans. After a while, the men started to notice that they were not getting their mail.

This situation presented itself as an opportunity for the African-American female battalion of women, to take up a new role and to travel to Europe.

In charge of the unit was Lieutenant Colonel Charity Adams. She was the war's highest-ranking African-Caribbean woman in the U.S Army at the time. The 6888 Battalion, (apart from the nurses) was the only female unit to be sent abroad from America.

The women worked around the clock; their teamwork, self-dedication, and a methodical attention to detail broke all records for mail and paperwork distribution to front-line troops in the war.

Although there was segregation in America with regard to black and white service personnel, they kept a record of the black personnel and their achievements.

Lilian Barder
Leading Aircraftwoman (Rank of Acting Corporal and Teacher)
Born in Toxteth Park area of Liverpool
Born 18th February 1918 - died 13th March 2015

Lilian Barder, a lady of dual heritage, was born in Great Britain, and orphaned along with her two older brothers at the age of nine years old and lived in a convent for many years away from her siblings. Her father had been a merchant seaman in WWI, and her mother, Lilian McGowan, was born in Derbyshire to Irish parents.

Lilian, the third of three children, lost her brother James, who was a seaman and was sadly killed. After a variety of jobs and experiencing some racism, Lilian decided to join the RAF. There was a range of jobs available, one of which was encoding and decoding signals.

Her choice of the RAF was due to her hearing disturbing stories on the radio of West Indians being turned down by the Army but being accepted by the RAF.

After a great deal of hard work, she became "Acting Corporal", and she met and married Ramsay Barder (also of dual heritage) in 1943, while she was still in service.

After her time in service, Lilian became a mother of two and went back to school and university to train to become a teacher.

Lilian Barder was one of the first black women to join the British armed forces. Very few women of colour who joined the services have been recognised, however, hers is the first name that comes up when speaking about black women who fought for Britain.

Cynthia Gittens

Cynthia Gittens
29th July 1935 – 2nd September 2015
The Queen Alexandra Royal Army Nursing Corps
Presented to Queen Alexandra
Recipient of Veterans' Medal

Cynthia E. Gittens was born on 29th July 1935 in Barbados.

Cynthia travelled to England when she was nineteen years old and joined the Army when she was twenty. During her time in service, Cynthia was presented to Queen Alexandra of Denmark, who was the wife of Edward VII.

The Queen Alexandra Royal Army Nursing Corps (QARANC) is a unit that has served at the sharp end of the military from the 19th Century. In fact, it can be traced back to the Crimean War, to Florence Nightingale. Queen Victoria had a hospital built for them in Netley.

The Royal Victoria Hospital opened in 1863 and takes care of Military personnel wounded in war zones.

Queen Alexandra was the president and died in 1925, at which point Queen Mary took over her role as president. All that remains of the hospital now is the foundation stone, which was laid by Queen Victoria.

Although the role of black nurses was overlooked, it was a job that was at the cutting edge where courage and humility were needed in the face of adversity.

When the rules changed and the women were allowed to care for white soldiers as well as black, they sometimes had to deal with some white soldiers who did not appreciate them. The nurses had to maintain their professionalism to put aside any negativity in order to give comfort to the dying, and help the sick to recover.

Interview

I met Cynthia Gittens at her home. She greeted me with a warm smile and invited me in. She came over as a very warm but complex person.

Cynthia joined the QARANC and served in Cyprus at the time of the brutal EOKA uprising in Famagusta. She remembers that when she arrived in Cyprus it was very hot, and as she stepped off the plane, she fainted. She said, "One night I was sitting outside with some of the other girls, chatting with five young men before they were due to go out on patrol the next day, only to be told in the evening that they had all perished. For me," she said, "that was the reality of war".

After service in the nursing corps, Cynthia retired, and adjusted into civilian life, but never forgot the brave men and women she served with in the war years. She passed away on 2nd September 2015 and will be missed by everyone who knew her.

Her photograph now hangs in a place of honour with other Caribbean personnel in the boardroom of the West Indian Association. She is sorely missed.

Her brother, Leroy Gittens, served with the Royal Hussars, Queen's Own Buffs, an infantry regiment of the British Army from 1961 to 1966.

Rosetta Young

Queen Alexandra Royal Army Nursing Corps (QARANC) & Princess Mary Royal Air Force Service (PMRAF)

Rosetta was born in Barbados (often called "Little Britain", due to its adopted English culture and its English ex-pat community).

She decided to join the armed forces, however, she thought herself too young to commit to the 22 years engagement of service. She joined the QARANC (Queen Alexandra Royal Army Nursing Corps) as a student nurse, aware that she would have opportunities to be posted overseas to other units, an aspect she found quite appealing.

After training with the army, her first posting was to Woolwich in England. She was also posted, after qualifying, to Germany.

During 13 years of service in the army, Rosetta rose through the ranks; first as a Private, then a Corporal, after which she applied for a commission and became a Lieutenant. Her commission in the army came to an end in 1980, by which time she had become a Captain. As her army rank of Captain was transferable and she could be afforded the equivalent of Flight Lieutenant in the RAF, she decided to join the Princess Mary Royal Air Force Service.

Her first posting in the RAF was to Lincolnshire, but she was subsequently posted to Cyprus. This was during the time of the Falklands War in the 1980s and she was commissioned to take care of the wounded soldiers returning from the battlefield, along with their families based in Cyprus at the time.

On ending our interview, Rosetta reflected on an incident that took place while she was in the army. It was the time when she was applying for her commission and had to travel by train from her base in Germany to HQ which was about 50 miles away. She spoke no German, and to this day, wonders how she got from the base to HQ and back again without getting lost.

She found herself sitting on the train opposite some Generals and Captains who were looking at her with amusement. One of them said to her, "You look very smart indeed; did you make that outfit "? She felt this was a bizarre comment, but realized that they had asked the question because they were unaware that there were black women personnel in the army.

Connie Goodridge Mark

This plaque was dedicated to Constance Winifred MacDonald Mark
By the Nubian Jak Community Trust

Born Constance Winifred MacDonald in Jamaica in 1923, she is known now as Connie Mark.

Connie had a very eclectic background. Her paternal grandfather was a Scotsman, her maternal grandfather was Indian and from Calcutta, her maternal grandmother was half-Lebanese, while her paternal grandmother was Jamaican.

Her father taught in a school for British army children, while she was privately educated at a girls' school that was a block or two from Harry Belafonte's home.

In later years, she was much in demand for her poetry and storytelling events. Brought up with a strong belief in "King and Country", she was once quoted as saying "We didn't grow up with any Jamaican things, we grew up as British".

Yet, once in Britain, it was her passion for the Caribbean that drove her to champion its culture and become a force within the black community.

At 19 years of age, she was recruited in Jamaica into the ATS (Auxiliary Territorial Service), working as a medical secretary in the British military hospital. She refused to accept a subservient role when one English officer tried to get her to act as her personal skivvy. She was eventually promoted to Lance-Corporal. After an incident where she believed that she was owed back-pay, she said, "The Queen owes me eight years of tuppence a day." It took a while, but Connie did receive the money in the end.

She married Stanley Goodridge, a Jamaican fast bowler, in 1952. She married again and became Connie Marks, the name by which we know her today.

Connie received her British Empire Medal for meritorious service in 1992 and an MBE in 1993. She knew Lilian Barder and would meet up with her and other women she had met during the war years. Connie passed away on 3 June 2007 aged 83. A plaque was placed on her former home in Hammersmith, West London by an organisation run by the Nubian Jak Academy.

Norma Best

Norma Best was born in Belize, on 20th May 1924. In those days, Belize was known as British Honduras. She was 20 years old when she joined the ATS (Auxiliary Territorial Service). She decided that she wanted to travel, and thought that joining the ATS would give her the opportunity to do so.

When she told her father of her intentions, he told her that he had served in Egypt in the First World War as a driver. This was a great surprise to her as his Army service was never mentioned in the house.

As a child and young woman growing up in Belize, she had studied the geography of England, and dreamed of being there. Reading books such as the Royal Reader taught her about England and nothing else, although Norma was well-read in other areas.

Her father pointed out that she might never get to England due to the German activity in the Caribbean Sea. "I don't care," she said "I'm going", and so she did.

On her way to England in 1944, the ship stopped at Jamaica. She remembers that, on the way over, the sea was very rough as there was a storm. There was very little to eat as the ship was tossing about so much that it became impossible for the cook to provide hot meals.

The next stop was New Orleans, where they were fitted for uniforms, and spent a week not being told of the exact date of their departure.

Eventually, they were ready to leave and did so on the Queen Mary. The journey fulfilled part of her dream and quest for adventure. For a while, she stayed in Scotland, where she had an uncle in the Forestry Unit, before moving on to London.

Norma started her service as a driver at the military training centre at Guildford, Surrey where she said Winston's Churchill's cousin was one of the instructors. She and the other girls said that they were treated very well there. In fact, they did a bit of teaching themselves, as the English girls there had only ever seen Africans before, and were amused at the variety of skin complexions of the Caribbean girls. It was her wish to become a driver, as her father had in WWI; however, she could not deal with the weather and opted for an administrative post, where she stayed for a year before being transferred to London.

Norma said that being in the ATS was a wonderful experience, and in fact, the only discrimination she met with was when she married her husband. He was in the Royal Navy and she had met him in Belize when he visited there. His Commander was against the marriage and drummed up a phoney charge against him in order to stop it going ahead. However, he was found not guilty and freed.

At the end of the war, Norma took part in the VE Day celebrations standing on the Embankment in London. She then decided to study to become a teacher and studied at Durham University. However, after qualifying in 1947, she was told that she would not be able to stay in Britain and must return to British Honduras if she still wanted to become a teacher.

She found whilst in Belize that she could not settle, and so returned to Britain where she married and had children. She then decided to go into teaching and became a headmistress of a primary school in the London Brough of Brent from 1961 to 1988.

Nadia Cattouse

Nadia was born in Belize, British Honduras in 1924.
Joined the ATS in WWII.

Nadia Cattouse was just the type of middle-class, well-brought-up woman the army was looking to recruit when they decided to allow women of colour to join the army. Her father was Albert Cattouse, the Deputy Prime Minister for British Honduras.

Nadia joined the ATS and was trained in Edinburgh to be a signal operator. While in the ATS, she also became a physical trainer.

By leaving the Caribbean to join the army, Nadia paved the way for the women who followed her, such as Norma Best. She was one of the first six female recruits from the Caribbean to travel to Britain.

The first stop-over, in Jamaica, was used as an acclimatisation exercise in preparation for Europe. She had to stay at a military base in the mountains for initial training before moving on to New Orleans. She then moved on to New York, before boarding RMS Queen Mary to Britain.

The Queen Mary was stripped down to the bare minimum during World War 11, in order to accommodate enlisted passengers, transport troops and prisoners of war. It was also painted camouflage grey in order to remain undetected at sea. Unlike most merchant ships that sailed in convoys during both World Wars, Queen Mary sailed without escorts.

After the war, Nadia returned to Britain. She had attended teacher-training while in Glasgow, so she had the grounding to become the headmistress of a mission school.

However, Nadia had many strings to her bow and returned to Britain in 1951 to fulfil her ambitions. She attended the London School of Economics. Later, she appeared in several television productions, including "Dixon of Dock Green" and "Crown Court". She was also a folk singer and recorded several songs, such as "Little More Oil" and "Beautiful Barbados".

Nadia eventually married composer David Lindup and had a son, singer and songwriter, Mike Lindup.

Corporal Collete Prince

Corporal Collet Prince.
Born in Jamaica
CMT (Combat Medical Technician)
A. Squadron – for Medical Regiment

Collet was attached to the front-line Ambulance crew as a Medic in Cyprus. In Kosovo, she taught basic first aid to troops. She was also an Army Counsellor, an MP (Military Police) and part of the DART Team, under Major Glen Lindsay in the UK, and qualified in 2004.

One of Collets' choices of work while in Jamaica was to join the Army. However, she was told that she would not be accepted as she was too short.

On arriving in the UK, a friend asked her to accompany him to the Army recruiting office, where it was suggested by the recruiting officer that she join. In her words, she said she told him that he was having a laugh as she was turned down in Jamaica for being too short; plus, there was the added fact that she was Jamaican.

The recruiting officer reassured her that they would take her if she passed the test, and that being Jamaican was not a problem since Jamaica was part of the Commonwealth; hence, she was able to join.

As a Christian, Collet found training challenging, having someone swearing at her while standing in her private space. She hadn't experienced being sworn at before. As a young woman, she had lost both parents but was very well protected by the church and her foster mother.

Collet's first experiences as a front-line Medic in Cyprus was difficult. She found herself having to deal with medical emergencies alone, with only a telephone link to the doctor as back-up. She also had to treat both soldiers and civilians alike with the most horrific injuries.

It was when she returned from her tour of duty that she joined the recruitment section of Aldershot, known as the DART Team. She also spent three years in Germany in the Welfare department.

Her experiences as a young woman, living in a man's world, as the army still is, could sometimes be challenging, but Collet is up for the challenge. Now, tasks such as having to go on an eight-mile run each day with a heavy-laden pack on her back are normal, as it is important that all soldiers, men and women alike should be ready for battle.

No special dispensation is given to the women soldiers so that if a heavy pack needed to be carried in combat situations, any soldier, male or female, could carry it effectively.

Collet is happy and feels that the army, to date, has been very good to her. She noted that the DART Team is one of the best things for a soldier. She said, "You learn about different cultures, diversity, and religions.

The Army states that you have to accept people for who they are, but how can you accept something you don't know? So that is why the DART Team is so important; it educates, and with Major Glen Lindsay at its head we are very fortunate."

Cheryl Thornley

Cheryl Thornley
Born in London
Joined the Army in 1994
Logistics Corps based in Pirbright

Cheryl Thornley joined the Army in May 1994 and went into the Royal Logistics Corps Training Centre based in Pirbright.She underwent Driver and Radio Operator Training at Leconfield, where she met her future husband, Kevin. Unfortunately, while in her first posting to Germany, she was given the nickname "nigger". At the time, she did not worry too much about it. She was eighteen years old, had never left home before and was a bit naive about the world. She knew it was not right, but she thought that it was normal for the Army and accepted that it was how things were. She said today, as an adult and barrister, "I can see now how unacceptable that behaviour was, and how it flagged up the more negative side of the Army at that time."

When she returned to the UK, Cheryl started a family and had to juggle the demands of being a young mother and a soldier. This was extremely challenging, especially when Cheryl was posted to the Former Republic of Yugoslavia (Bosnia) with the NATO Stabilisation force. Being a young mother away from her family was hard, especially during challenging times such as coming under fire and changes to the main supply route, where Cheryl later discovered the daily convoys had been misrouted over live IEDs (explosive mines) and it was pure luck that these had not detonated causing her to lose her life at such a young age. Cheryl later received the NATO Medal for her services in the Former Republic of Yugoslavia.

Cheryl was a keen Regimental Athletics Champion and competed in the National Army Athletics Competition in the 800m, 1500m and 4 x 400m.Cheryl Thornley left the Army in 1998 to join the Police with an Exemplary Record of Service. She spent 20 years in the Police service, gaining commendations for excellent investigation work and two Queen's Jubilee medals for service to the Crown.

While in the Police, and as a busy mother of three children, Cheryl gained a first-class Law degree and a scholarship award to study as a barrister through the Inner Temple. She was the first black female to be called to the bar by the former Head of the Crown Prosecution Service, Director of Public Prosecutions, Sir Ken MacDonald.Cheryl now works as a lecturer in Public Services, passing all her valuable experience and knowledge to the military personnel and police officers of the future. She also runs her own coaching, mentoring and personal development business.

Not only is Cheryl an extraordinary woman, but she is also my niece, and a role model for any young black woman. She has, at a young age, trained and studied for three professions successfully, married a fellow soldier and had three children, while running a home, a job and a business. She has demonstrated that "you can have it all".

George Phillips

Joined RAF 1958 at 21 years old.
Served until 1970

George Phillips arrived from Barbados in 1955, at the age of 18 years old. While working as an electrician in London he decided to join the RAF as a means to travel. He was young, tall, handsome, and lived in London where all the action was, and he wanted to be part of it. He was 21 years old when he joined the RAF in 1958 as Ground Crew.

I asked George how he felt about wearing the RAF uniform. He said that he felt proud as it meant something, fit like a glove and there was a certain sophistication about it.

George did his training at Winslow near Manchester. When they arrived, the weather was terrible, especially since they had to march from the station to the barracks in the snow, something that they had not experienced in Barbados. The next day, they were taken on an early morning run, which was performed in only a tee-shirt and shorts.

I asked George if there was a lot of camaraderie with the other guys when he joined. "Yes, "he said. "There were a lot of black guys from various islands and they all got on well".

However, he recalls an incident that took place not long after he arrived at the camp. It was noted that when given leave, he and his black colleagues on their return to the camp were challenged and physically searched, ID was also asked for. However, when his white colleagues returned to camp, the guard on duty would say, "Hello blondie, or "Hello Jock," and just waved them through.

This was unacceptable to George and the other guys, and so they complained to the highest level. This protest did bring change. It was decided that the guard in question was not fit for the job and was removed.

George's job was to service the planes, such as the Vulcan Bombers, the Argosy and Beverley.

Although he was trained to service helicopters, to this day, he has not done so. He trained in many stations including RAF Marham, Finningley, Aden,

Khormaxkha, Brize Norton, and two years in Cyprus. On the whole, his training went well.

George has many stories to tell, including his trips to town while in Khartoum, dressed as a native, and holding hands with his comrade, (as was the custom between the locals). This was done in order not to be detected by the enemy. He experienced fights with GIs who thought he was from the U.S. and was stealing their newfound girlfriends while in the U.K.

George's story is a love story also, as he met his wife at a dance in St. Pancras in Kings Cross. It was the custom, particularly for young men and women from the West Indian community, to go there to dance every Saturday.

I asked George about his wife and what were the circumstances of his meeting with her. He said it started as an unfortunate situation as he was supposed to meet someone else and he was stood up.

He then decided to go to St Pancras Dance Hall at King's Cross, which held a dance which many Caribbean civilians, soldiers, and RAF personnel frequented. As he walked in, he saw his future wife, Andrea. He thought she looked quite attractive and asked her to dance. She accepted and they ended up dancing with each other all night.

They had, however, little time together before his leave ended and he was posted off to Cyprus. He asked to accompany her shopping the week before he left. As they were passing a jeweller's, George asked Andrea which ring she liked, and she asked if he was sure? "Yes," he said, and with that, they went in and chose one.

It was a wedding ring; he then suggested that she tried it on, and when she did, he asked if she liked it. "Yes, are you sure?" she asked. "Yes," he replied. After this, he told her that he would be leaving the next week and he thought that they should get married. It was then decided that they should. Today, they have been married for over 60 years.

I asked George what he would say he had taken away with him from his experience of being in the RAF. He said that he came away with a lot of good experiences, accumulated good buddies, who learned from each other, irrespective of nationality or age.

After working for 20 years with London Transport, George is now retired and living with the woman he married due to love at first sight from that night at St Pancras Dance Hall.

Steve Blizzard

Major Steve Blizzard
Blizzard entered RCAF in 1960
Qualified Doctor, and Jet Pilot

Major Steve Blizzard said, "I joined the organisation in London, England in late 1952 as an ex-member of the Edinburgh University Air Squadron".

He then entered the RCAF (Royal Canadian Air Force) scholarship programme in 1960 and qualified as a doctor in 1963, becoming an RCAF Medical Officer.

After further training at the RCAF Institute of Aviation, he went to Moose Jaw RCAF Base where, unusually for a medical doctor, he qualified as a jet pilot on the T-33. He was known as the only Trinidadian medical doctor who was also a qualified jet pilot, and was attached to N0. 414 Electronic Warfare Squadron until 1969, after which he returned to Trinidad on leave of absence. While in Trinidad, he ran a Light Aeroplane Club, training students up to licence standard.

In 1975, Steve Blizzard returned to Canada and the RCAF (Royal Canadian Air Force) after deciding that the opportunities for someone with his qualifications did not exist in Trinidad.

A Squadron Leader by this stage, he served on the RCAF staff as a senior Flight Surgeon up to his retirement in 1984, while continuing to preserve his links with the RCAF cadets.

In 1992, he was inducted as a member of the prestigious International Academy of Aviation and Space Medicine, an organisation whose membership is limited to 250 worldwide. In the meantime, he had become the Director of Civil Aviation Medicine in Canada and a senior consultant to the government on all matters of aerospace medicine.

Then, in 2003, he was awarded the Edward Warner Award of Aviation Medicine which is the highest award in the world that any flight surgeon can attain. Squadron Leader Blizzard's career in aerospace and aviation medicine should serve as a beacon for many decades to come.

Squadron Leader Dr Stephen V. A. Bizzard now lives in Canada. He said: "I knew many of the boys who joined up in WWII, including those who remained in England. One who remained was Percy Lewis, my friend from elementary school, who became a boxing champ over there. He still lives there, and we correspond to this day.

Another friend was Frank Dowdy, economist, recently deceased in Trinidad, who was still a pilot in the RAF when I met him in a nightclub in London in 1948. Another RAF member who returned home and did well was Fitz Bell, my wife's cousin, who became a Permanent Secretary.

Ulric Cross, of course, was my hero in WWII, and still is to some extent, and I clearly remember the reception held for him at the Prince's Building.

Today, it is nice to know that I am held in such high regard."

Philip Kelshall

1944 - Posted to 169 Squadron
Flew Mosquito's
Then 29. Night Fighter

Philip Kelshall joined the RAF at the beginning of WWII. He was selected for pilot training and passed with an above-average grading, which almost automatically meant that he would be used as an instructor.

After he completed his instructor's course, he was posted to the RAF College at Cranwell, where he instructed new pilots in flying eleven types of aircraft.

In 1944, Philip Kelshall was posted to N0. 169 Squadron, an element of 100 Special Operations Group, where he flew a Mosquito on night missions protecting the main bomber stream by disrupting the German night fighters. At the end of that tour, he was posted to 29 Night Fighter, with the job of ranging over Europe during raids, attacking German night fighters, particularly around their bases.

After the war came to an end, he returned to Trinidad and became a second local pilot in BSIA. He progressed to be Chief Pilot, then Operations Manager, Ops Manager Technical and finally, the first local General Manager or Chief Executive of the airline, a post that he held from 1963 to 1968, during which time he introduced the Boeing 727, the airline's first pure jet aircraft.

Philip Kelshall came from a military family. His uncle was in the Civil Defence Authority in WWI, and his cousin was Lieutenant Commander Gaylord Kelshall.

Lt. Commander Gaylord Kelshall

Gaylord Kelshall was born in San Fernando in 1940. His cousin was Philip Kelshall, who flew Mosquitos in WWII.

His father participated in WWI and was O.C. in the Civil Defence Authority.

Gaylord's first job was as an Operations Officer with British West Indies Airways (BWIA) in 1958. He acquired his first pilot's licence in 1963 and became the first pilot of the Air Wing of Trinidad and Tobago Coast Guard in 1964.

Gaylord Kelshall was a prolific writer and wrote many books about the history of Trinidad. We discussed this when I interviewed him at the Chaguaramas Military Museum in Trinidad. The museum is also the home to an actual Tristar L1011 Airbus, formerly owned by BWIA. and is said to be the only such aircraft on display outside of an airport in the world, which Gaylord was very proud of.

The Museum holds items that would have been used in WWI and WWII, along with other artefacts from, and highlighting Trinidad's aviation past. The museum played a great part in Gaylord's life and he spent a lot of time improving it, and cataloguing the airmen who served in the Wars.

Gaylord Kelshall obtained many awards such as: -

International Military Author of the Year award.
Gold Hummingbird Medal 1918
Gold Charonian Medal 2003
Recipient of the National Trust Heritage Preservation Lifetime Achiever Award 2011

Leroy Gittens

Enlisted: 1962 in Barbados.
Regiment 13/18 Royal Hussars - Gunner and wireless operator. Queen's Own Buffs, as a Tracker in Borneo. Became an Historian, and at Lectures at the Imperial War Museum - Ex-member Serviceman's Association.

In the 50s and 60s, the British Army found that it was short of men, and so it sent recruiting officers to the West Indies to recruit young men for the forces, of which Leroy was one.

They painted a great picture for the young recruits. They told them that they would be able to travel and learn a trade, which would set them up for life. They also said that they would be treated the same as any other British soldiers. The sound of this appealed to Leroy, and his expectations were high as it was the 60s and, in his words, "no one was killing anyone".

Because it was the practice of the British forces to recruit the best from the West Indies, the test that the recruits were given was much harder than the one given to their peers in England, even though the men who joined from the West Indies did so as volunteers.

The exam that they took allowed them to join the prestigious Royal Hussars Regiment, of the famous" Charge of the Light Brigade", as it was one grade up from the exam of the foot soldier.

Leroy Gittens was recruited into the Army in 1962, and trained at Catterick in Yorkshire. He was 20 years old. At this point, the army was transferring new recruits from the West Indies to England by chartered plane, in stark contrast to some of the Caribbean soldiers who fought during WWII and had to pay for the fare themselves.

Unfortunately, when he arrived in England, he was disappointed by the way they were misrepresented by the recruitment officers who visited them in Barbados. After being told that they would not have to take the exam again, they discovered that comments made on their official records did not reflect that they had already taken an exam in Barbados. Instead, it was made to look as if the men who arrived from the West Indies were not clever enough to take the exam in England, and so were excused. The true fact of the matter was that the men in the West Indies had a higher level of education than their English colleagues, many of whom could not read or write.

While in the Royal Hussars, Leroy realised that they were only going to be posted in England and Germany. This was disappointing as he wanted to travel the world.

After some thought, and a word with a senior officer regarding his future, he put in for a transfer. At that time, he was in the Armed Corps as a wireless operator. In order to travel, he had to find a regiment that was travelling afar. He was told that there was one that would be going to Hong Kong in two weeks. However, they were infantry (foot soldiers) which, for him, as he put it in his own words, meant he had to "demote himself", which he did and requested that he be transferred to The Queen's Own Buffs.

The Queen's Own Buffs were a regiment that was travelling to fight in various theatres of war, which appealed to Leroy.

The regiment went to Hong Kong and Borneo, at which point Leroy was then deployed as part of the Tracking Teams which were sent for training in the Malaysian jungle. Each team consisted of eight men and Leroy was the only West Indian in his team. Leroy found the training invaluable and relates how every pebble, leaf, and footprint told a story. Once training was complete, they were deployed to Borneo.

This involved working with dogs. The dog handlers abseiled from helicopters with their dogs on their shoulders, thus enhancing trust and a bond between the dog and its handler. One of Leroy's jobs was to watch the dog handler's back and cover him through the jungle.

His expectations were now being fulfilled as he was being able to travel and see more of the world. They got on well with the villagers who were only too willing to share some of their knowledge of the jungle with them.

Leroy tells the story of being in Borneo, on patrol, and coming across a village, where at one time in history, there had been head-hunters. They found a path which had stakes embedded in the ground on both sides, with human skulls on top. One of the other guys asked the Chief of the village about them and was told that when the Japanese passed through the village, they were very brutal to the villagers and gave them a hard time. The villagers knew that they had to return the way that they had come, and so it was decided on their return through the village, they would pay them back for their cruelty, hence the heads on the pikes.

At one point, Leroy had been dispatched to the U.S. Army for duties with the United Nations at Panmunjom, which is between North and South Korea. He was aware that there were sections of the GIs who showed hostility to black soldiers, however, he managed to hold his own and finish his tour of duty with them.

Leroy was posted back to Hong Kong for some time before returning to England.

After the war, Leroy settled down into civilian life and became a part of the West Indian Organisations founded to promote ex-servicemen. He also gave lectures on the subject at the Imperial War Museum. He still gives lectures today, and has a wealth of military history information.

Leroy is on the far left of the group photo and on top of the vehicle

Ian Bruton

Squadron Leader Ian Brunton
from Trinidad Qualified as a Pilot in 1962
First Pilot to fly as Captain in a V bomber

Ian Brunton joined and qualified as a pilot with the RAF in 1962.

His first posting was as a co-pilot in N0. 57 Squadron, where he flew as a co-pilot on the Victor B1 V bomber. He moved through the ranks quite quickly and so his next posting found him as a Captain in N0. 214 Squadron, flying the Victor B1.

Brunton was the first Caribbean airman from Trinidad and Tobago to captain a V bomber, at that point, his rank was Squadron Leader.

This was such an improvement on what was going on in WWII, when Caribbean airmen were not allowed to fly planes that had a full complement of men, for fear that they would not have the confidence in the pilot because he was black. Brunton retired in 1976, but not before he had toured as a flight instructor at RAF Leeming.

He returned to Trinidad and joined BWIA (British West Indies Airways) where he flew as a captain and rose to be a Fleet Manager. During this time, as with most airmen, he took up the law and became the only practising lawyer who flew as a commercial pilot. He accumulated more than 15,000 hours and, while continuing with his flying, he was appointed as Chairman of the new Civil Aviation Authority in 2000.

Ian Brunton continued his quest for advancement and knowledge. Forever moving forward.

Dennis T. E. Olivier

Born – 19th December 1945
Royal Air Force Tactical Signals Unit
Senior Aircraftsman

Dennis Olivier was born on 19 December 1945 in Port of Spain, Trinidad and Tobago. However, as a boy, he joined the Air Cadets in Birmingham, England.

He trained as an RAF Boy Entrant Telegraphist at No. 2 School of Technical Training, RAF Cosford, from 17 May 1962 to December 18 1963. After this, he attained the rank of Corporal Boy Entrant.

After training, Dennis served in the RAF from the 18th of December 1963 to the 18th of December 1972, at which point he had attained the rank of Senior Aircraftsman.

When Dennis told his parents that he had received his posting to the RAF Steamer Point, Aden in 1964, his mother promptly proposed that his remaining service in the RAF be "bought out", which meant paying off the Air Force for over eight years of service. She could not bear the thought of her one and only son going off to a war zone. Dennis and his father disagreed. As a single airman, his tour of duty was, in fact, fixed for two years.

Dennis said, "The first negative experience of Aden was when I arrived at breakfast at the Britannia Club, London, where we spent the time in transit on our way to the Middle Eastern Theatre.

I opted to join another military person as company for breakfast, but I noticed the soldier who was sitting opposite me twitching painfully and uncontrollably. In conversation, he explained that he was on his way from Aden to a military hospital in England to undergo treatment for bullet wounds he had sustained in Aden. Immediately, I sank into a mild depression. Here I was, on my way out, and he was returning with serious injuries received on the battlefront. My first thought was to return home and inform my mom that she should proceed with the transaction for my 'buy out' of service.

Having overcome the apprehension and thought, I faced Aden with a different perspective, one of survival and serving my time. From the first day of arrival at RAF Steamer Point, the countdown for returning to good old Blighty started. Daily, one would strike one day off the calendar while reciting the cliché, "days to do getting few."

November 1966 marked the ending of my Aden tour. For twenty-two months, I had been very vigilant and cautious in my movements. I had escaped two bomb explosions on the base, two nail-bomb explosions in restaurants, one grenade attack at a Christmas Party and one bazooka attack at our local cinema. I was beginning to feel claustrophobic, so I ventured out to the local cinema.

After the show, I was returning to base when I heard a metal object hit the ground. At the same time, a white Mercedes Benz flashed by. A soldier raised an alarm with a loud shout of "Grenade!" I dived to the ground almost simultaneously, landing face first.

My whole life flashed before me in seconds. I was merely a foot away from the grenade. Luckily, it was disarmed by a heroic soldier. Seconds later, I felt a boot on my back as a military policeman shouted, "Get out of here." He was moving those closest to the grenade. "Although the grenade was prevented from exploding, my face was all bloodied and bruised from the dive. I truly had a narrow escape.

"The army, through various theatres of war, allowed me to visit many countries, including South Yemen, Aden, East Africa, South Arabia, and Singapore to mention a few, countries I would not have seen otherwise."

Dennis served in the Royal Air Force Tactical Signals Unit – 38 Group from 1971 to 1972, and was awarded The General Service Medal with Clasp "South Arabia".

He also received a medal, 'The Remembrance Medal', by the African Caribbean Memorial Foundation on 11 November 2020.

For his work and dedication to the welfare of the ex-servicemen of Trinidad and Tobago, he later became the Chairman of Trinidad and Tobago Federation of the Veterans' Association from 2006 to present.

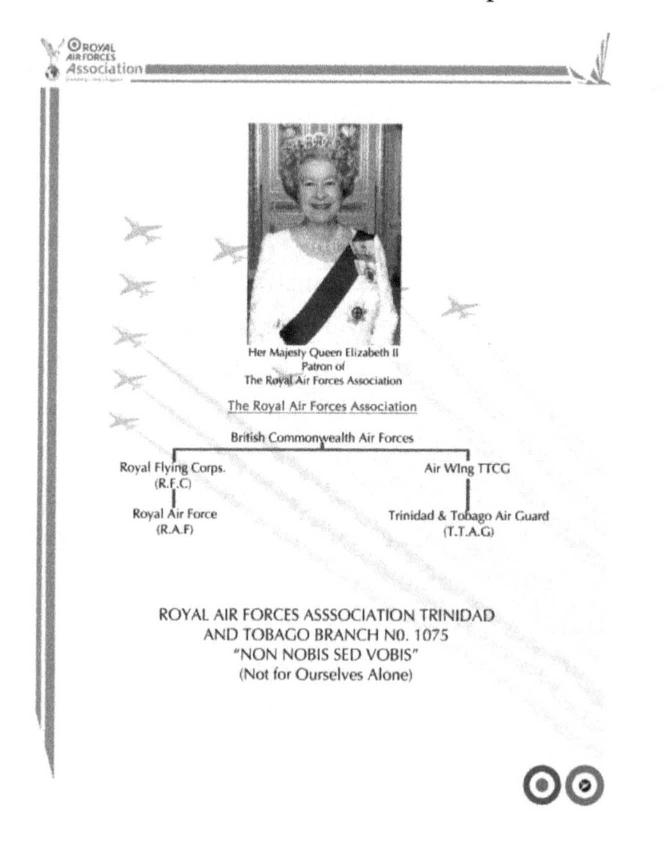

Peter Daley

Born 1956 in Birmingham of Jamaican Parents
Green Jackets 1972

Peter Daly joined the army as a boy soldier in 1972.

Not being old enough to fight, he had time on his hands and so the army trained him in any and every weapon they had, including mortars, and anti-tank weapons.In late 1972/73, two young 17-year-old lads died while fighting in Ireland. This caused a furore, as they were not old enough to vote but they were old enough to die, it seemed, for King and Country.

After this incident, rules were changed and soldiers then had to be 18 before they could go out and fight and vote.

The training that Peter received was to prepare him, and the other soldiers, for life in the battalion. Before going into a battalion, he was posted to Wales where he did his final week of training, which entailed mock battles and learning to do drill.

Peter had joined the Green Jackets (light infantry) and was in number three battalion. He did not join the Army for the Mother Country or Queen and Country; he was born in England and joined because he wanted to. The first battalion had a significant body of black soldiers, numbering 30 or so.

The second battalion had less than 5. This meant that if you were a black soldier and in that battalion, you were on your own, with all that entails, including name-calling and bad treatment at times. The third Battalion, which Peter was in, had 52 black soldiers, and things were more manageable.

He was posted to Berlin where, along with the first battalion Para of Wales, American and Russian soldiers guarded Rudolph Hess on a three-month rotation, three months on, three months off.

Rudolf Hess was born in Alexandria of German parents, who toasted Kaiser Wilhelm on his birthday with a glass of wine even though they were not living in Germany at the time and had made their money through colonial trade in Alexandria. Later, Hess became Hitler's right-hand man, henchman, and deputy.

He flew on his own to England and crashed-landed just outside Glasgow, avoiding being shot down. He was trying to get to the Duke of Hamilton, whom he had met once before.

Hitler was unable to comprehend what Hess was doing, so he told the German people that Hess was suffering from being mentally deranged and suffering from hallucinations. This, he said, explained why and what he did.

Peter explained that Rudolph Hess had the best treatment money could buy in prison, sometimes even better than the soldiers who were guarding him. For instance, if he died while the Russians were guarding him, they would have to go into Berlin, which was in the west, as they would want to leave the prison as a memorial, while if he died under the English, their mindset would be to just blow it up and get out of there.

Hess was allowed to walk around the grounds freely. The soldiers, however, were not allowed to talk to him but he was allowed to talk to them. However, there were some people who spoke to him. He then replied through his minder. They knew that they were running a risk as if they were caught, they themselves would end up in jail.

Peter described Hess as 6'3" with a full head of black hair. He had a minder and the doctor with him at all times. The soldiers walked above him on a ramp watching his every move.

When Hess died, it was a relief to most of the soldiers guarding him. The American soldiers indicated that they should just shoot him, so they could go home; that way it would be done and dusted. Others suggested that he should just do away with himself. Of course, none of these suggestions was adhered to.

In all, Rudolph Hess lived for 13 years in Spandau prison. There were other prisoners who were there, however, he never met them and they never met him.

When Peter left the army, a lot of his colleagues from the Green Jackets joined the Sultan of Brunei's army. However, he went into recruiting, education, and working in youth clubs. He also worked as a social worker and with Dr Barnardo's Home for troubled children. He followed this up by working for local government with regards to housing.

Peter gave lectures in schools regarding his experiences and the service. He was shocked on many occasions to discover that the children in the schools believed that black people came to Britain on the Windrush, and did not participate in WWI or WWII. They did not know that there were black soldiers, pilots, navigators or sailors.

He did say, however, that he would have no objections to any of his children joining the services, as long as it was of their own free will.

He pointed out that Britain is still recruiting people from the West Indies today and, in fact, they recruited a large amount to go to Afghanistan. However, after their tour of duty, they were not allowed to stay in Britain.

At this point, I asked him what he thought about this; he expressed his unhappiness about it because, in his mind, he felt that it was unjust to take people from another country, make them battle-hardy, and then after they've done the job for you, send them back to another country for that country to deal with the problems, although he pointed out there might not be any problems, of course.

We know today that many soldiers who have been in the theatre of war came out suffering from various elements, mental and physical. Taking that into consideration, how much harder would it be for someone who has to go back to their country, after experiencing death and fighting in war zones, to no job and perhaps nowhere to live or no family to assist them to integrate back into that society?On ending the interview, Peter pointed out that there is a body of older soldiers who have a story and need an audience to tell the stories to. I found that comment quite moving.Peter Daley is another ex-soldier who has spent a large proportion of his time after service trying to educate young people, black and white, as to the history and the contribution of Caribbean servicemen and women, and should be commended.

Trevor Edwards

Fighter Pilot

Trevor Edwards

Flight Lieutenant

RAF

Jaguar Pilot - 54 Squadron 1997

British Airways Airbus Captain.

Flight Lieutenant Trevor Edwards once said, "When I wear jeans and a T-shirt, I get stopped by the police. I mean, I don't look like a fighter pilot, do I?"

Today he is a commercial pilot and, although times have changed, that aspect of his life is still a reality for many black men walking the streets of Britain.

Trevor Edwards was born in Woolwich, East London, of West Indian parents, and grew up in a tough housing estate, but attended the Grammar School in Dartford and worked hard. Trevor joined the RAF in 1985 as a Regiment Officer, whose task was to defend RAF Airfields. During training, it became obvious to him that the best job was that of a pilot.

As a working-class man, he had no idea of what was required in order to pass the selection process as a pilot in the RAF. His assumption was that all fighter pilots were public school-educated, Caucasian males, who were quick-witted, and had private incomes.

Trevor's route to becoming a fighter pilot was first to get transferred out of the RAF Regiment and onto the Flying Training Course, which was almost impossible.

The RAF Regiment had already taken its toll on Trevor. The infantry course lasted six months and led to him getting frostbite in his feet, which turned to gangrene, resulting in him having to have all ten of his toes amputated. He was so determined to achieve his goal that he considered this to be a small price to pay when looking at the bigger picture.

While in rehabilitation at RAF Headley Court, where Trevor was being taught to walk again, he met Barry McKenna, a Tornado Wing Commander.

Barry McKenna convinced Trevor that his injuries were no bar to him becoming a pilot. He was aware that Trevor had acquired some pyrotechnics for his RAF Regiment contracts, so he convinced his Squadron in Bristol University to give Trevor ten hours' instructional flying, in exchange for some pyrotechnics.

Trevor did very well during his flying instruction and received a very favourable training report, which was sent to the pilot selection board at RAF Biggin Hill.

Although medically unfit to continue as a regiment officer, Trevor managed to convince the doctors that he was capable of flying an aircraft. The result was a position on a flying training course and a subsequent transfer to aircrew.

In 1987, he started his flying training at RAF Swinderby, receiving his wings the following year. He was top of the class when he took the Tactical Weapons course and was soon posted as a fighter pilot, flying Jaguar planes, to join 54 Squadron at RAF Coltishall.

Trevor's time as a fighter pilot was eventful. His squadron was deployed to Turkey several times to enforce the "no-fly zone" over northern Iraq, as well as being deployed to Southern Italy.

Every once in a while, Trevor would catch himself being amazed at the fact that a lad from East London had grown into a fighter pilot, flying a Jaguar carrying 1000lb bombs, with guns armed and ready to go. A real-life "Top Gun".

Eventually, Trevor left 54 Squadron to complete the flight instructors' course at RAF Scampton. He was then posted to RAF Linton-on -Ouse where he instructed student pilots to fly the Tucano aircraft. He stayed in the RAF until 1997 when he left as a Flight Lieutenant to become a commercial pilot.

Trevor Edwards is now a Captain for British Airways.

In August 2017, Trevor appeared on a television programme called "Giving Back", in which he was reunited with one of the Jag fighters he flew. Once again, he met the man who inspired him to continue with his goal to become a pilot, regardless of the disability of losing all his toes.

Kadmile McFee

Kadmile McFee – Joined Army
2001 Recruited in ST Vincent
Parachute Regiment
Trained at Pirbright – Based at Aldershot. Joined the Parachute Regiment Tour - Ireland, Iraq, Basra, Lebanon

I interviewed Kadmile at the Army Association office. He was very tall, had fine features, broad shoulders, a refined voice, and looked you straight in the eye when speaking to you, and he was very direct in answering any questions put to him.

When he spoke, it did not take long to realise what an intelligent man he was. He had a wealth of knowledge, and was able to speak on any subject pertaining to the army, not only about it, the ethos of today, but of its history.

I was quite impressed at his memory recall, and his ability to paint a perfect picture of what he was describing when telling his story, to the point where one would be transported to the scene.

I asked Kadmile what motivated him to join the British Army, so he then told me a story of "The Iron Man".

He said, "The Iron Man was a statue that was in the main square of the town on the island of St Vincent. It represented war veterans, those who died in WWI and WWII, and others who survived. It encapsulated their dignity, courage, integrity, loyalty, self-confidence, self-discipline and ambition.

The issue surrounding the relocation of the war monument to an obscure location in a park was considered by the locals as an affront to the men who fought for Britain and should have involved the consensus of the electorate, the people, in fact, who had voted Prime Minister Mitchell into office. While acknowledging that the political climate and architectural beauty of the country had changed, he said, "The people felt that the Prime Minister could no longer connect with the statue, and saw it as ancient history, while in England, for instance, they honoured their war dead with Veterans' Day, Remembrance Day and memorial services."

He went on to tell me about a protest made by an old soldier who stood to attention in front of the statue in the square, while saluting, for a day and night. That image stayed with Kadmile, and projected the dignity, staying power and courage that he hoped he could experience one day if he joined the services.

The British Army sent a recruitment officer to St Vincent to recruit 700 army personnel, however, they were only able to recruit 400 at that time, of which Kadmile was one.

The recruitment was only carried out if the person in question was able to pay their own fare to England. In fact, it had to be a British Airways return ticket.

I asked Kadmile what would happen if they did not have the money. He said, " It was simple; if you could not pay your return flight to England, you could not join the army. However, they did say that they would defer your recruitment for seven months, to give you time to find it."

Kadmile said that he asked the officer, Major Bradley, what the situation would be in relation to living in England after they were out of the army? He said, "I can never forget what he said; Join the British army, join the culture, become part of Britain, become British, you are British".

To clarify what he had said, Kadmile said, "So I can take it that I become a British citizen"? The major said, "It's not up to the army whether you become a citizen or not, but look at it this way, you are not going to live in Britain all your life and not live a life. You are going to have kids, you're going to get married, so you are British. However, when you come out, it's a matter between you and the Home Office, but I can't see any reason why you would not be able to stay, given the fact that you have served in the army."

I asked Kadmile what would happen if he got injured, would he have to go home? "Yes," he said. "You might have a pension, however, it would not be enough to meet all of your medical and housing needs."

After training, Kadmile became part of the 7th Parachute Regiment, Royal Horse Artillery. He said that instead of being deployed straight away, they were sent to work with the Fire Service who had gone on strike, so they had to work with what we know now as the "Green Goddesses"(military fire appliances) to help put out fires in the city.

Then they had the call; they were going to be deployed to Kuwait. They called the camp Eagle Camp, a name the guys made up, as it was not yet a fully functioning camp. They were sleeping on the ground with no tents in temperatures of 40 degrees each day. After four weeks in that environment, they started to put the tents up, and a camp started to be formed. This was because the political situation was not quite formed when they arrived.

It was 1.30 am when the alarm sounded, Kadmile said. "We were going to war." He continued, "At the same time as the alarm was going off, you could hear the fighter jets, hundreds of them, a combination of British and Americans. The sky was full, all planes heading towards Iraq. We were told that we were going to Iraq and that it would take four hours to get there. However, it took eight hours, due to the large sand dunes and general terrain.

Every so often, we would hear "Gas, Gas, Gas". We would then have to put on our nuclear and chemical warfare clothing, ready for a gas attack that never came; this went on for 28 days. At one point, we had the clothing and respirators on for 9 hours. This made the going very hard, due to the temperatures in the desert, and sweating.

After a run-in with the Iraqi National Guard, we were left trying to get through burning oil fields. We could not see through the smoke, we couldn't drive through the flames, so it was decided that we would have to be airlifted over the fields.

We could hear the Apache and Chinook helicopters coming towards us. They were coming to uplift the guns. We got into the helicopters, and the Commander then said, "Okay, lads, this is it; we are going in."

The helicopter was flying at top speed, so as not to be shot down. The noise was such that they couldn't hear themselves think, especially when the helicopter was making tactical moves.

Kadmile said, "All of a sudden, you are screaming at the top of your voice, although you cannot hear yourself. When looking at the other guys you know that they are doing the same because their mouths are open. You start to be lifted out of your seat. The only thing that is saving you from falling out of the helicopter is your seat belt. Even your gun is floating away from you, and you start to find it difficult to catch your breath.

Due to the speed of sound, when the helicopter levels out and you stop screaming, you start to hear the echoes of the screams coming back. However, you don't have the time to be enamoured by it, as the next thing you know is that you are on the ground and being bombarded, from left and right. Shells were coming in everywhere. As a gunner, I went into action straight away, along with the other gunners."

"As I fired, I knew it was not a practice; it was real people I was firing on. As I did so, tears flooded my eyes; I didn't want to cry, it was the emotion that took me over. I knew that they had all been wiped out, 1000 people."

After that encounter, the Iraqis were on the run.

Kadmile was in the thick of it, and also described a 'blue on blue' situation. This is when your own men shoot on you, thinking that you are the enemy. That particular situation was shown on the news the next day.

Kadmile's next tour was in Basra for twelve weeks where he was faced with constant bombardment from mortars, and fighting with the Taliban. He was then posted to Lebanon, where they were sent to remove U.K. and Canadian nationals, ahead of a conflict which never materialised. This was followed by training for Afghanistan.

At the end of his story, he hits you with the shocking tale of his partner's attempted suicide, his son being taken into care while he was away fighting, and the army's refusal, after seven years of service, to give him compassionate leave. He returned to the U.K after buying himself out, to find he had lost everything, even the right to stay in the country.

Major Glen Lindsay

Major Glen Lindsay
In the Army for 36 years
1st Tour Falklands
Royal Artillery – Bombardier/Corporal
Joined the Commandos, supporting Royal Marines
Officer Commanding the Diversity Action Recruiting Team
Born in Jamaica in 1955, and moved to UK in 1965.

Major Glen Lindsay, born in Portland, Jamaica on 14 May 1955, emigrated to England in 1965, aged ten, to join his parents in Harlesden, London. They moved to Birmingham a year later, where he completed his secondary education and enlisted into the army in 1971 as a junior soldier aged sixteen.

Glen had seen an advertisement on the television, where the man in the advertisement said, "Join the army to see the world, it's a man's life". He ended the advertisement by saying the army needs YOU, while pointing to the viewer on the other side of the screen. As an impressionable 16-year-old, this seemed appealing and stayed with him for some time.

At that time, after leaving school, most guys were expected to either go for further education or an apprenticeship and then get a job.

Glenn wanted independence and decided that the army would be able to offer him that.

He had no expectations or any great career plans when he joined. He was recruited in Birmingham and then went for two years to the Junior Tradesman's Regiment in Scotland. He found that to be what one can only call an experience. He was away from home for the first time and had to experience different behaviours, different attitudes, and having to conform to various things other than his previous experiences.

As he was always a very disciplined child, he basically just got on with things and took everything in his stride without question. Although, in his own mind, he did try to see the rationale behind all of the different requirements.

Glen cannot remember seeing any other person of colour for a very long time. Eventually, there was a young lad who joined, and what amused Glen was that he had a Scottish accent. A black man with a Scottish accent? At first glance, he thought that he was putting it on.

At 16 he was not eligible for deployment and would have to wait until he was 18 before that could happen. However, he had decided that since he had not seen any black people up to that time, when he moved into what was then, to him, the man's army because he would be 18 and there continued not to be any people of colour, he would leave. After all, he had come from a black country, which was Jamaica, and he had lived in Birmingham where he'd seen people of colour, so it was a bit of a shock to him that there were no people of colour in the regiment. And he truly believed, at one point, that he was the only black person in the entire army.

However, when he was deployed in the regular army in Germany, there were 20 to 25 black men in his company, who were functioning and doing all the things that he would have expected them to be doing. This was very important to him, as he needed some sort of social stability.

While interviewing Glen, I asked him what he thought or felt about being in Germany, since the ethos of Germany in the Second World War was that of murder and supremacy. He said that he never thought about it as he was never taught it as a child. He had completed two years' training at Junior Tradesman's Regiment Troon in Scotland, achieving the rank of Junior Bombardier (Corporal), before he was posted to 39 Regiment Royal Artillery in Sennelager, Germany, where he was employed as a Driver/Radio Operator in the Regimental Command Post.

However, what he did notice was that, once you learnt the language and understood what they were saying, it transpired that the Germans were incredibly prejudiced, especially the older ones; the younger ones he felt were much better, however, he said that he was not interested in the Germans or Germany. What he was interested in was his unit, the black men in his unit and what military life was all about.

After six years, during which he was promoted to the rank of bombardier, he applied for and successfully completed, the All Arms Commando Course, embarking on a new and exciting adventure, with deployments on a majority of operational tours including Northern Ireland, the Falkland Islands, Iraq (1991), Afghanistan, and Iraq (2003).

After Glen left Germany, he went on to Northern Ireland.

I asked him how he felt about some of the Irish asking black soldiers to come over to their side, as they felt that they were also an oppressed people.

Glen pointed out that they were in Ireland to do a job, there was no socialising with them, and that it was work. He continued to say that if you allowed yourself to be taunted by them in order to distract you from your mission and think twice about what you are doing, it would only have been counter-productive and so he never gave it a second thought.

Glen adjusted himself to the requirements of the army to get on.

To that end, he would take on the challenges, take promotions, seriously progress fast, and get the recognition. He knew that, if he applied himself, it was doable.

Looking back at Walter Tull, who was an officer and led his men in the First World War and died in the Somme but never received his medal because of his colour, I asked Glen if he thought that there are many issues with relations to being in charge of men of both colours in the army today.

"Oh no," he said. " In the army, my experience is that if you have made the grade and you have established yourself, and you're bedded in the knowledge of the system, they know you, and you command the respect of people at that point, I think colour and race go out of the window. Except for the ignorant few, but they have got to be forgiven. British soldiers receive some of the best training there is. I would recommend the army to any young man or woman today."

Major Glen Lindsay has travelled widely, deploying on many demanding training exercises in countries including Kenya, Canada, Gibraltar, the Czech Republic, Jamaica, Norway, Egypt, Denmark, Germany, amphibious training in the Mediterranean (on a ship), Turkey, Belize, and Oman.

A self-motivated and keen sportsman, he started boxing at the age of sixteen at regimental and club level, participating in the junior ABA as a light welterweight. He is also an accomplished middle- and long-distance runner on road, track and cross-country, and a qualified AAA middle- and long-distance running assistant coach.

Training and operational commitments abroad took him away from home for long periods of time over many years, but he is blessed with a dedicated and loving family.

During his thirty-six-year career, he was promoted through the ranks of the army to the rank of Major, reflecting his drive, ambition, determination, and dedication to the service.

Glen said that the army is a career choice, and you have to join for the right reasons and be dedicated. To do it half-heartedly means that you would not be able to stay the course.

Major Lindsay commanded the Diversity Action Recruiting Team. Part of the remit of the DART team was to train new recruits to learn about the cultural differences of the soldiers within the army to help promote closer working relationships and bonds. He would also go out into different minority communities, promoting the many diverse career opportunities on offer in the army, a job he had been doing for at least ten years of his service.

He has worked his way up through the ranks and is a perfect example of how high you can get in the armed services.

After thirty-six years in the army, Major Lindsay has now retired and is putting that same determination, know-how and skills, when dealing with people and projects, into his civilian life, making himself a force to be reckoned with in the commercial arena.

Alan Barrett

Alan Barrett
Born in United Kingdom
The Parachute Regiment
Air Cadet/Boy Soldier

Alan Barrett's motivation for joining the army was that of watching films on TV as a boy. Some of his school friends were in the Air Cadets, as he was. Alan joined the Cadets when he was twelve years old. The required age was thirteen, but he wanted to join so badly that he lied about his age. It would have been a natural progression for him to join the RAF. However, he failed the test, and since most of his friends had joined the army, and he had been watching the Falklands war on TV, he decided that he would like to become a soldier.

One day, one of his friends went to the Army Recruitment Officer to collect a travel warrant from the recruiting officer and Alan decided to keep him company. While waiting in the office, the sergeant suggested that he have a go at the recruitment mock test while he was waiting for his friend.

He took the test and he passed, so the sergeant then suggested that he returned and take the real test, but before doing so, to speak to his parents and see what they thought about it. He did so and they agreed.

Alan was trained at Aldershot in the Browning barracks for 22 weeks. Of the 80 of them in the platoon, three men were black. However, after two days, there were only two of them and following two weeks, the other one left leaving only him. This was due to the daily racism.

There were also physical altercations however, that went right across the board. It didn't really matter what colour you were in that environment; there was always going to be physicality.

Alan knew what to expect because he had friends that were already in the army and they had spoken to him about it, so he knew that bullying was par for the course. He felt that the fact that he was in the cadets also gave an insight into the life or tensions that you would be involved in within the army or the Royal Air Force.

He had joined the Parachute Regiment, a regiment that had a reputation of being one of the best. This meant that, as people achieved higher ranks, they felt as if they had to live up to that particular rank and behave in a certain way, which in some ways was tough.

This training was basically a test to see how you were doing and how the candidates would cope under pressure. Situations were all filmed, as it was important that they got the right people and they got the training right. For instance, there could be a daily situation where you could be sitting on the train with people going to work in their suits and holding briefcases in their hands, while you would be in full uniform with a gun in your hands.

Alan's first tour was in Northern Ireland so, before he left, they did what was called "The Northern Ireland training". This consisted of them patrolling dummy villages, containing various scenarios that you would encounter, such as having to deal with aggressive people approaching you with bombs and shooting at you.

Alan arrived in Northern Ireland in the time of the troubles, when there were bombings on the mainland and also in Northern Ireland, so there was a feeling that you were in danger before you even got there.

When Alan arrived in Northern Ireland, he was under 18 so he wasn't allowed to go onto the streets. This meant that he had to stay in barracks and do chores until he was 18 years old. However, as he didn't know how to drive, he was taught by another black colleague in Belfast.

They would drive through Belfast in an unmarked car with a pistol and rifle hidden within the car in case there was any trouble. He did this until he was able to join his colleagues patrolling the streets.

As a black man, most people reacted to him by just staring, especially if they were patrolling in a rural area because for some, the only time they saw a black person was on TV. The odd person would speak to him at times.

He remembers the time when he was crossing a field with his colleagues and the cows in the field started to charge them, at which point the farmer appeared and deliberately approached Alan as he was the only black soldier there. After singling out Alan, he proceeded to call him all the black names under the sun. Alan and the other seven soldiers basically told him where to go and proceeded across the field.

When seen out on patrol, young men would approach the black soldiers and give them leaflets which said, "This is a white man's army. What are you doing in the white man's army? Come and join the IRA". From their point of view, the black soldier wasn't seen in quite the same way as the white soldier was; he was someone who should be with them as a race as they also were oppressed.

Alan said, "Depending on the area of the town, you would know what to expect; if you were in an area that was considered to be bad for the soldiers, there would be Irish flags and certainly murals on the walls of the houses. You knew straight away that there would be trouble. Some people would shout at you and throw things in order to get a reaction. If they were able to get one, they would start throwing petrol bombs and a riot would begin. The soldiers knew that too, so they would just basically ignore them as far as possible".

Alan explained that Northern Ireland, in the time of the troubles in the 1980s, was a very dangerous place. It was a place where you had to keep your wits about you at all times and even bite your tongue at times, as provocation was around every corner, something which after a full day of patrolling, being on high alert and being abused, was not always easy to swallow. However, as soldiers, they knew that they were there to do a job.

There was a particular verbal abuse situation, where Alan's Corporal stopped the patrol and asked Alan what he wanted to do about it. Alan was then given the nod to go ahead and confront one of the four men who were aggressive and abusive towards him.

Eventually, the man backed down. However, by then, a crowd had gathered around the patrol and started to throw batteries and petrol bombs at them. The patrol was able to radio for help while being pelted, and when the vehicle turned up, they all got into it. However, the crowd started to rock the vehicle from side to side while a rain of petrol bombs and batteries continued to shower the vehicle until it was able to make an exit with everyone safely inside.

Alan also went to Cyprus and Belize where he had jungle training. He was quite excited as he was English and had never been to a black country before. He found the jungle quite formidable with its deadly spiders and snakes and having to sleep at night in it. However, he did enjoy that particular training.

I asked Alan if he found that he had any difficulty in obtaining his first promotion. He said that since he was part of a boxing team and really was quite fit, it was suggested that he joined the RTI course. In order to do so, he had to have a certain rank, so he was given a temporary rank of Lance Corporal. However, after leaving the course on completion, he was able to maintain and keep the rank. Although it was easy for him, it was not always easy for other soldiers of colour.

On leaving the army, as Alan held the rank of Corporal due to his good character and standing within the regiment, although it was the rank that he thought that he would have acquired long before the time he did.

It is Alan's belief that, even today, joining the army for a young man can only be a good thing, as it has changed immensely over the years and it's a good place to start as regards discipline, and achieving one's goals.

Stanley Roy Archer

Gunner/ Driver

25th Field Regiment Royal Artillery

Born in the hills of St Mary, Jamaica in 1932.

Tour of duty in Cyprus, during the uprising of the Greeks and Turkish Cypriots for independence.

Stanley was one of the first to be recruited in 1956. Stanley said, “It was considered that twelve weeks’ training was all that was required in order to train a young man before he was sent off to kill and be killed for the Mother Country”.

While in service, Stanley acquired the nickname ‘Dan Archer’ after his namesake on the BBC Radio 4 programme, The Archers and that character. Even the officers called him Dan Archer. He was one of two black men in the whole battalion.

He felt that the British had learnt nothing from WWI, and made a point of giving a class of new intakes lessons on how to brush their teeth, and at what times.

The Greek and Turkish Cypriots were fighting for independence from the British as well as for unity with Greece, while the Turkish Cypriots were totally against the idea. Hence, in 1955, Britain declared a state of emergency in the month of November. This led to the Greek Cypriots establishing EOKA (Ethniki Organosis Kyprion) meaning (National Organization of Cypriot Fighters), supported by Archbishop Makarios. It was a very dangerous time.

According to the records of a House of Commons' sitting on the 31st January 1956 (ref1 page 176), there were already 7,800 men doing their National Service out there.

In 1957, Stanley was sent to Cyprus, where the civil war between the Greeks and the Turkish Cypriots was in full force. Eventually, an agreement was reached and they were forced to share the island.

By the end of the 'emergency' on 31st March 1959, 35,000 British troops in total had served in Cyprus. Questions were also being asked of Mr Anthony Head, the then Secretary of State, whether 12 weeks of basic training was enough to prepare young lads for their experiences in Cyprus, in comparison to other services, like the police.

Stanley and other men from the Battalion were not allowed to mix with the locals, due to the possibility of them being shot or blown up; of course, they knew of men who had been killed.

Stanley said, "Many of the people in the villages were Muslims so we were not allowed to look at the young girls. Of course, there were always the exceptions, of men who did not understand or want to adhere to the culture, which ended up with a bit of a stir and everyone being confined to barracks in order to defuse a dangerous situation".

Being black was not an issue in Cyprus, Greece or Turkey, as there were always black people there.

Stanley said, "One evening the medical officer and I were stopped in our tracks as we were about to tuck into our meal. We were ordered to drive down Murder Mile, so-called as it was where you were most likely to be shot at and killed, and rescue a top high-ranking Colonel and his driver who had come under heavy fire; it was unknown at the time who was wounded, the driver or the Colonel.

I drove as fast along the stretch as I could; the bullets were hitting the vehicle fast and furious. On arrival at the spot where the Colonel and his driver were, it was decided that I should send off a smoke flare to signal for a helicopter to uplift the driver, who was seriously wounded. We were later to find out that he did not make it; in fact, the flat canvas stretcher we had placed him on to ferry him to the helicopter had been so bloodied that it had to be burnt".

As for the Colonel, he was already deceased on the scene and was loaded onto another stretcher and secured by Stanley at the back of the jeep, while bullets flew around them.

Just as they were about to leave, Stanley was asked if he was Gunner Archer. "Yes," he said. He was then handed a blanket with something in it, which turned out to be the Colonel's foot. Stanley then threw it into the back of his army jeep, while kissing his teeth followed by a few Jamaican expletives.

On the way there, the Colonel managed to end up on the road, at which point Stanley had to get out from behind the wheel, collect him, and put him back into the jeep, while all the time, bullets were flying around him. In so doing, he was risking life and limb, for a man who was already dead, and he was at risk of finding himself in that position also.

Lester Hendricks
Mr. Lester Hendricks – RAF. Ground Crew Construction Querent Lester joined at the age of 17 years.
RAF Ground Crew Construction Querent Equipment Section Joined in 1944 aged 18 years old

Lester volunteered to join the RAF at the suggestion of his aunt. He was young and ripe for adventure so he agreed. In the back of his mind, however, he remembered a map on the wall at school, which was a map of Jamaica with chains wrapped around it. As he knew the history of Jamaica involved the slave trade, the map represented the bonds that were placed around Jamaica at that time. It was generally felt that if the Germans won the war, Jamaica would find itself enslaved again, with the chains being that of Germany, so it was an added reason for him to join the RAF.

It was Lester's first experience of the sea and a large ship. He promptly became seasick; however, that was surpassed by the fact that they were travelling in formation within a convoy. The convoy was the assurance that they would reach England safely as they could have been fired upon or sunk by an enemy submarine.

Lester's first impression of England was a pleasant one.

As they travelled, they were told about the schools, rugby pitches, and given a general summary of the English countryside, which he found exciting, and in his words, he "was up for it". He enjoyed everything about the war and did not think of the possibility of being killed.

There was a large contingent of Jamaicans on the ship; however, once they landed in Yorkshire and then went on to West Malling in Kent, they were joined by men from Guyana and Barbados. Lester said that, although there were quite a lot of English boys there, all the West Indian boys were billeted together.

RAF West Malling Station's motto was "Portam Custodimus" (The Gate-Keeper). In 1940, it was in the front line against the Luftwaffe. It became a full-force training school for the RAF staff in 1944 when Lester attended.

It was discovered that he was not very good at unarmed combat and was unable to drive. His job was to look after the uniforms and equipment. As it turned out, no one was sent to war while he was in the RAF and in that particular camp.

He returned home in 1947, while many men stayed. He was young and he missed home. At eighteen, before he left Jamaica, he did not realise that life in Jamaica was hard; he now knew that he had made a mistake by going back. He would now have to save the money to return to Britain.

Some men who had farms had received money on their return to Jamaica to help them out, however, as Lester was young and had just left home, he was only given the £28.00 which was a week's wage.

Lester returned back to Britain in 1955. He then married a Jamaican girl and had two children. His wife's parents eventually borrowed money on the land that they owned to fund his passage back to England. He then sent for his wife and children at a later date. Unfortunately, after eighteen years of marriage, they divorced.

Lester then started working on the buses, but he never discussed his 20+ years of service in the RAF with anyone. He then did 'the knowledge' and became a black cab driver, before marrying again.

One of his sons went into the army and was there for 22 years, and was sent to Northern Ireland in the thick of the troubles. Then on to Germany, with the peace-keeping corps, where, after becoming a staff sergeant, he became a warrant officer. He had one child who then went on to Birmingham University.

Lester's' daughter married an English man and their only son went on to Cambridge University.

One of the reasons that Lester did not mention that he was in the RAF, he said, was because he felt that he did not do much. However, he feels now that through his son going to Northern Ireland and his service, his son did what he was not able to. Furthermore, as his daughter was now a teacher, and her daughter went to University, they have all become valued citizens in Britain, and so he feels now that he has made a positive contribution.

I think that the fact that he was ready to fight was a contribution in itself.

After WWII

After WWII had come to an end, most West Indians believed that they could stay in Britain if they wished. However, the general consensus of the government was that they had to go back to the West Indies. While some emigrated to other countries, such as America, a few were able to stay in England, with some even re-enlisting in the forces.

Ex-servicemen returning to the West Indies remembered how difficult it had been for the returning injured soldiers who came home after WWI. They had no home and no money for medicine. The pensions that were promised by the British government did not materialise and there was no work, to speak of, for them back at home.

At the end of WWII, history was repeating itself again as many ex-servicemen from the army, RAF, ATS, and some nurses, found it difficult to settle back into their old jobs, on returning home.

After the war, Britain was on its knees. It had been devastated by the Blitz. German bombs had destroyed not only residential areas but also factories and fundamental systems and services necessary for the economy to function. Whole streets were burned out and deserted and many people sheltered from the elements in dangerous structurally unsound buildings propped up with huge planks. This situation continued well into the 1960s.

It soon became apparent to the British Government that Britain was in crisis. Most of its men had gone to war and many had died or returned injured. Of the remaining population, many of them were too old to rebuild the infrastructure. Britain needed an injection of people to provide the help they needed and they looked to the West Indies to be that help. An invitation was sent out "Britain needs you!"

When the call came from Britain once again for help, taking their situation into consideration it was almost a given that many would return, so a number of ground crew, navigators, pilots, and nurses once again paid their fare and returned by way of the ship called the Windrush.

The vast majority of West Indians came to Britain with a plan - to work and to earn enough money to send back to provide for their families back home and return to the Caribbean within five years. However, for a variety of reasons, many never returned.

When these men and women arrived from the West Indies, they came with qualifications and expected to find jobs to suit their skills. For the most part, this did not happen. Many of the first arrivals were only accepted into the armed services because they were highly educated and had careers in the West Indies such as teachers and engineers. They also acquired further skills in the armed services.

They found that they had to take up jobs that the British did not want to do. They also found that now, they were no longer looked on as the war heroes they were, but were treated with suspicion, distrust, and hatred. The British public couldn't imagine that the man driving the bus or sweeping the streets may have put his life on the line for Britain.

There was a sudden realisation that now they were out of danger and the war was over, these men were black and foreigners. Many of the new arrivals were greeted with cries of "why are you here?" or "why don't you go back where you came from?"

When the Caribbeans first arrived in England, they were taken to different parts of the country. Some were taken as far as Wales and Scotland. Some found their own way, as they had friends already in England. Others went to London where they were taken to Clapham South where they stayed in old air raid shelters, crammed in together, one on top of each other, in bunk beds.

What was very evident, but is never talked about or noticed, is that every man who came back on the Windrush wore a suit, shirt and tie and hat and had polished shoes to finish off his look. Women wore their Sunday best, dresses, gloves and best hat. This was not a people who were lacking in pride in themselves, their appearance or ambitions, and despite the conditions they were forced to live in, they still maintained their smart appearance.

Those that were taken to Clapham were then taken to Brixton to the Labour Exchange to get jobs. Hence, they did not gravitate to Brixton, they were taken there. For those who found jobs in the area, the next thing they looked for was accommodation in the area near their jobs. Today, Brixton is being gentrified, and so they are being priced out of the area.

Finding accommodation was difficult because there were signs up that read "No Irish, No Blacks, No Dogs". This meant that people slept in basements, at exorbitant prices, ripped off by those who would exploit them by making them sleep three or four to a room.

It was clear that the government was not going to help, although many English people in the 50s lived in council houses provided by the government.

The only accommodation that they could get was that of dirty dank basements, which they had to leave before daylight, or a dilapidated room with peeling paper on the walls, an outside toilet, and a stove on the landing, which was used by many. So, after they realised that, the people of the Caribbean decided to buy their own homes, and rent rooms out to each other until they could all afford to buy their own homes.

In order to raise the funds to buy property, groups of West Indians would come together and form a partnership scheme (otherwise known as 'Throwing a Box'. They would agree to all pay in an equal amount into a kitty per week until they reached a target amount; for example, they paid £1 per week until they had each paid in £100.00. When the kitty reached £100.00, as long as they continued to pay their contributions, the first person could withdraw their total to put towards a deposit for a house. When the kitty reached £100.00 again, the next person could take out their lump sum, and so on.

This scheme was very successful. It built a sense of community and trust and many West Indians were able to raise the deposit and hence buy a house this way. Eventually, government intervention and jealous neighbours put a stop to the scheme.

What the government did do, however, was to give them jobs, although not necessarily the jobs that some of them had expected as skilled men with qualifications. They could not ask them to dig trenches or roads as they had in the war, but London Transport did take a big campaign to the West Indies enticing people to come to London to work on the trains and buses.

Women, in particular, were also recruited in the West Indies to come to Britain to train and work as nurses in the then-new NHS. Others worked in factories. The West Indians took whatever jobs they could get to survive.

There was such a shortage of labour in Britain at the time that, if someone was treated poorly or not paid well enough, they could walk out of their job at 10 am and walk into another one by 2 pm.

In the early 50s, the newly arrived West Indians didn't have just the shortage of good housing to contend with, they also had to acclimatise to severe winters with high snowfall, dense freezing fog and very dangerous roads. Some ex-service personnel might have got used to the weather but not necessarily adjusted to the strange old wives' tales about black people.

It was believed in England that it was lucky to touch a black person's hair, and many West Indians found complete strangers rushing up to them and touching their hair, while others had their hair touched just out of curiosity. The Caribbean's were dismayed at the lack of respect this showed, but in most cases laughed it off.

There was also the myth that black people had tails which had to be removed when they came to Britain. People would touch West Indian people's bottoms to see if they had a tell-tale 'stump', especially British ladies when dancing with West Indian men.

It wasn't just the British who had an incorrect view of the new West Indian immigrants. Many West Indian people's perception of Britain was based on what they saw in films and read in books. Britain was supposedly a land of rich, sophisticated, well-educated and well-spoken people who lived in large houses and wore beautiful clothes. However, post-war Britain was a different place.

Britain was not just a place of fog, snow and coal fires. For some people, the cities were bombsites; places where people left their laundry on the doorstep to be collected, washed and returned later that day, known as the 'bag wash', because no-one had washing machines or space to wash and dry clothes. Children used to collect bottles to sell and cash-strapped people would gather old clothes to be weighed and cashed -in for money.

When Caribbean people saw British women on their knees, washing their doorsteps with their heads tied up in headscarves, they realized they were no better than them and no worse.

Many people believe that black people only started to immigrate to Britain from when the Windrush arrived. In fact, black people have been living in Britain for centuries. However, "The Windrush Generation" is considered to be ground zero from where the achievements of black British people should be judged.

It should be noted that through hard work, the first, second and even third generations of post-Windrush Caribbean children have progressed in life, going to University and doing well for themselves. Of course, in every society, there are the ones who make the headlines.

For young black people, there are many role models. They just have to look for them; they are there.

Johnson Gideon Beharry VC

Private Johnson Gideon Beharry VC
Born 27th of July 1979 in Grenada
Awarded the Victoria Cross,
Britain's highest award for bravery.
Princess of Wales's Royal Regiment

Johnson Beharry earned his Victoria Cross while based in Al Amarah, Maysan Province, Iraq, in 2004. Private Beharry is the first person to receive the Victoria Cross since 1982 and the first non-posthumous British Forces recipient since 1965.

His Victoria Cross was earned for two separate acts of valour under fire in the town of Amara, near the southern Iraqi city of Basra. First, he was struck in the head by a bullet while rescuing his comrades in an ambush.

A month later, he rescued further soldiers but suffered serious head wounds in an assault by a rocket-propelled grenade that left him in a coma and he was not expected to live.

Johnson was an armoured vehicle driver, responsible, as he put it, for the lives of those who travelled in it.

Interview

(Valour under Fire)

I interviewed Johnson Beharry at the Pirbright Army base. There were five of us in the room at the time.

Johnson told me that on his first attempt to join the army, he was refused. He said that he was disappointed but determined to get in, as he was determined to change his life, as he felt that he was not where he should have been and could do better.

He was told to go away and come back in six months. However, six weeks later he was back, with testimony that he had made an attempt to change his life and was ready for army life. He was worried at this point, as he came across the same person that had refused him the first time. However, out of sheer determination and passing the test, the army decided to accept.

I asked him if he could tell me what had happened to him, and why he was awarded the Victoria Cross, but only if he felt that he could or wanted to tell me about it. This is his account of the events:

He said, "While in Iraq on the 1st of May 2014, one of the patrols had gone out, and had asked for assistance. I was then asked to assist. The route was blocked by something in the road. Normally, we would just drive over it. However, in places like Iraq, you have to take a chance to drive over any obstacles. We looked for an alternative route, however, there wasn't one. The enemy had blocked our route in order that we would be redirected to where they wanted us to be, which was straight in line for an ambush.

Even when the vehicle got hit the first time, I didn't know what had happened and, in fact, I shouted back to one of the guys, "What's happening?" but no reply came back.

There were several bangs, five or six, then I realized that the vehicle was on fire, and I had no communications with anyone; I was in the middle of an ambush. Insurgents were coming from all different directions, and there was a wall in front of me blocking the road, so I just couldn't get out. Eventually, I was able to sort it out myself. I saw an opening and thought, "I can just leave the vehicle and go". Then I thought, 'Well, these guys depend on me to bring them out and to take them back to camp, so I can't.'

I stayed in the vehicle and tried to move the wall by ramming it, but the engine was on fire and I was losing power. However, I was able to move the vehicle slightly to the right and pushed the wall open as if you were opening a door; there was a space and I got through.

Now I faced a mine in front of me; I thought, 'If I go over it, we will all die', but then I thought, 'we're all going to die anyway'. We were under attack from heavy rocket grenades. So, I thought surviving that mine was 50-50 but what is happening here is 100%. So, I drove over the mine with the knowledge that I would die, but I knew I would be saving 30 soldiers. So, I positioned the engine of the vehicle over the mine, hoping that the engine would take the full blast and then I drove over it. We survived. However, I was now driving down the road into a killing zone, but I had no choice.

Then I saw something coming towards me and moved away but there wasn't really anywhere to go, so I moved back in line and thought, when it gets near to me, he'll stop or swerve away. However, as it got close, I realise that it was a rocket and I closed the hatch, but before it could be closed completely it was blown away.

Everything was coming at us; machine-gun fire, rockets, everything. I suddenly saw the rest of the company. The vehicle itself on the right-hand side was starting to glow red so I was concerned that the vehicle was about to blow up. I was also mindful that I had high explosives on board which included about four boxes of grenades.

I decided it was time to get out so, I drove the vehicle into another as it would not stop on its own. It stopped. On doing so, the Commander in front of me said," What are you doing"? I said, "This vehicle is about to blow, and I have casualties in the back. I need help. He said, "Okay". He then said, "You need to take it back to where you just came from". He then closed the hatch.

After a while, I realised that nothing was happening so, I thought, 'That's 800 m behind me'. I knew he was a Major but I was thinking, 'The vehicle was going to blow, but you are telling me to take it back'. I couldn't question what he was saying because he was a Major and I was a Private. So, I turned the vehicle around.

I eventually saw my chance to hand the men over to another vehicle. I got out of the vehicle and was now lying in the dirt outside next to it, with the knowledge that I had six people inside the back. So, I put my weapon on my back and I climbed up. The first person I saw was my boss. I spoke to him but got no reply. I pulled him up and put him on my back. I then went back to collect the others. In order to do this, I had to go through the engine cover, which was on fire, as there was no other way that I could get to them or get them out. After putting them in another vehicle that was safe, I then went to the back of the vehicle in order to get the others out, while under fire.

I got into the burning vehicle and started to drive back the way I came. As I did so, there was a company of soldiers to the left of me and I thought, 'If this vehicle goes up now everyone will be killed'. So, I went around the side of the building. I disabled the vehicle itself so that the enemy could not use it. I then went back on top of the vehicle and the disabled weapons system. While I was doing all of this, we were still under enemy fire.

I took three weapons out of the vehicle and ran into another vehicle and sat in the back. I could hear the Commander saying to the driver, "Drive, drive!" However, there was no response from the driver and he wasn't moving or saying anything. I jumped out of the vehicle and ran to the front to get the driver out so that I could take over as the driver had frozen. However, as I shook him, he came around and said that he could not drive because the back door was open'. Johnson said that he had left it open when he jumped out to help. He then ran to the back of the vehicle and closed the door, at which point the driver drove off without him.

All that Johnson could remember after that was that someone was taking his helmet off and pouring water over his face, and saying, "Stay with me". Johnson had been shot in the head. The bullet had hit his helmet and partially got stuck in it, thus saving his life.

"A day later I discharged myself from the Medical Centre, due to the number of big flies that were there."

I pointed out that he was shot up yet he was worried about flies, and everyone in the room laughed. "The thing is," he said, "I hate flies and roadkill".

However, he was told to go back because he had heatstroke, and was going to be sent back to the UK. He was told, two heat strokes and you're dead.

Johnson was determined to stay and fight for as long as he was standing, so he requested that he go in the back of the vehicle instead of driving. Due to his persistence, this was granted. He was told that he was not to get out of the vehicle if they came under enemy fire. He agreed. However, that did not last for long.

Six weeks later, Johnson was out on patrol when there was a detonation six inches from his face; he was able to reverse the vehicle to save the guys in the back but became unconscious and could not remember any more.

This incident ended his active army life and nearly took his life. His forehead, eye, and nose had to be rebuilt, and he suffered other life-changing injuries.

I asked Johnson what he thought about his life now. He said, "I didn't ask for the life I have now, it was given to me; but I know what it is like to have the ability but not have the opportunity, I know what it is like wanting to do something but you cannot do it, and just as I know what it is like to not have anything, I know what it is like to have everything and lose it. So, I guess I am only 30 years old, but years ago, I had to grow up and then when I was 24, I had to grow up even faster because I was put in a position I never ever dreamt about even knowing about. Even when I was handed the Victoria Cross, I didn't know what it was. Really, that's how bad it was. I had to grow up quickly."

I asked him if he had ever sat down and thought about what he has done, and what he has achieved, or whether it was something that he's just walking along with, as it were? He said, "I think that I'm just walking along with it. Hopefully, though, I'm using it for the right reason to help people like me".

"Everyone sees me walking around with a big smile on my face, but I am going through a lot of problems mentally. I still have a lot of pain, every day, in my head, shoulder, pain in the back of my eyes, because my eye socket is new. But what I can feel is where the plate joins the bone at the back of my eyes."

"I am just a soldier, but when I am in my uniform wearing the medal, I am a different person, as in I respect a huge part of this country's history."

"However, what is important to me is the contribution I made towards the lives of 42 soldiers. That is really what the Victoria Cross means to me. History never ends".

Today's Soldiers

Members of the DART Team at Pirbright

Corporal Graham & Foxy

I interviewed Graham, Foxy, Edward, Adam, and Clair at Pirbright Army base. The meeting of several Caribbean service personnel was organized for me with the help of Charles Heath Saunders of the army.

I asked them why they joined the army and what their goals were.

Graham

Graham said that he had always been ambitious and felt the army would give him new opportunities to progress. He said, "Since I joined, there have been no limits for me. The longer you stay in service, the more you can see what you can do." After doing a tour in the Gulf and four in Iraq, Graham is now training the next generation of recruits to the army. He feels that there are many opportunities for them, in regard to skills learned and confidence.

I asked him about promotion and whether he found it difficult to obtain. "For me, it is a double-edged sword. It depends on what trade you choose to take up. That is what determines the scope as I see it".

When he started, he did not understand that, so he had a slow start. However, he felt that whatever you put into the army, that is what you will get out of it. He said: "Don't just do what is required of you, do requirement plus. This is what will reap rewards."

Foxy

The army for him was a vehicle to develop skills that he already had, reaching full potential. He has also been in the theatre of war.

He observed that sometimes when people join the army, they feel that the whole world owes them something. Those people never last. He felt that the army presents you with opportunities, and you have to grab them with both hands.

He said that sometimes when he wakes up, he cannot move as he has a knee problem. However, as soon as he puts on his uniform, he is energized and ready to go.

Adam

Adam was looking after his family, as his home situation was difficult, but with his mother's blessing, he joined the army. It has given him confidence and enabled him to move forward with his career in a more positive way.

He admits that he still has a lot to learn, but he is willing.

Edward

Edward said that the army has changed all aspects of his life. “It makes you realise what you could have done in the past, and gives you an opportunity for finding a new direction, while giving you the confidence to do so.”

One of the things that he finds very rewarding is meeting people from other countries, and learning about their way of life.

I asked all of the DART Team what they felt about having women in the army. Did they feel, naturally, that they had to protect them, or did they feel that they were all soldiers, doing different jobs and you just had to get on with it?

The general consensus was that the women had to go through the same training as the men. They would be mentored for the first month, after which, they would take their place in the ranks.

Graham noted that very soon after they arrived, you would see who had potential, and you would give them a bit more attention, however, that would be the same for the men.

Commonwealth Day

Each year there is a Commemoration Ceremony on Commonwealth Day, at the Memorial Gates, Constitution Hill. Representatives of all the services meet to remember the contributions made by the people of the Commonwealth in time of war.

Each year the Prime Minister of the day attends the Commemoration and gives a speech. Reflecting on the contributions made by the people of the Commonwealth. This is followed by various speeches by several other dignitaries, ending with a prayer, and a buffet.

Lest We Forget

Today there are many black organisations that are springing up, in order to promote and remember the brave men and women of the Caribbean who left their country at a very early age, most paying their own way in order to answer the call of Britain to help her in her hour of need.

These organizations and individual pioneers of black history, many of whom work tirelessly in the background, are today bringing the contribution of the West Indian servicemen and women into the limelight. At long last, black people are beginning to tell their own history. They are now becoming victors, as we know it has always been the victor who wrote our history.

Nubian Jak – Produces blue plaques for buildings that once were associated with the black pioneers of this country.

Limelight Magazine promoted black servicemen for many years.

There are black army associations that keep a register of black servicemen, along with giving support. There are now university students researching black airmen and their stories, one at a time.

The RAF is to be commended for their efforts to promote their black pilots and aircrew.

The Imperial War Museum had an exhibition on black servicemen and women.

Several writers, including myself, contributed to a book about the lives of our servicemen and women called "Remembered" in memorial.

BWIR Flags

Paraded through Birmingham in remembrance of the British West Indian Regiment

The WAWI Project has researched and brought to life the Standards of the West India Regiment to bring forth England's forgotten history, give credit and educate a nation.

Horace Barnes
Of the WAWI Project formed in 2009
During a presentation by the Lord Mayor, 17th July 2011
for work in the community.

Horace Barnes is the driving force of replicas of the flags on display in Westminster Abbey. Above, he is receiving an award for the work he has done and the contributions to his local area and the wider community. The WAWI Project has researched and brought to life the Standards of the West India Regiment.

The meaning of WAWI is "Why are West Indians" in this country? The reason is quite simple; Britain called and they answered.

The Project reproduces flags of the WIR (West Indian Regiments) the originals of which are in Westminster. Many who walk beneath the flags there will not know of their origins. To increase awareness and the history of the flags and Regiments, the WAWI parade, with flags held high, along the streets of Birmingham, in honour of all those who came to help rebuild Broken Britain. And it is an opportunity to remember the sacrifices made by all communities, regardless of colour, creed or race.The parade is showcased at certain times of the year, to promote not only awareness but also pride. "Lest We Forget".

They are supported by organisations such as the BAPA, Black and Asian Police Association who through their team spirit and community engagement, continue to support the WAWI Project.

Conclusion

Some of these stories have never been told until now, some had been forgotten, and some overlooked. The story of the Caribbean in wartime has, for the most part, been written out of history.

Some of the people in this book have already passed away, some have already left the army, or started a new phase in their lives within the service.

However, it does not mean that their stories or experiences are any less important than on the day they took place. We should remember their contributions and the fact that they were volunteers, and so did not have to go to war.

I hope to have demonstrated with these stories, that despite all the hardship, and the danger they faced, the fighting men and women of the Caribbean were willing to make sacrifices in order to keep us safe and protect our democratic rights. This has not been in vain because we will not forget them, but we will remember their heroism.

We need to tell these stories in order to move forward, together.

Interviews – Primary Sources

Squadron Leader Ulric Cross – DSO - DFC - Audio and Film – London & Trinidad
Leroy Gittens – Audio & Film
Stanly Archer – Audio & Film
Lester Hendricks – Audio & Film
Rosetta Young – Audio
Major Glen Lindsay – Audio and Film
Sam King – Audio & Film
Alan Barrett – Audio & film
Johnson Beharry VC – Audio & Film
Gaylord Kelshall – Audio and Film - Trinidad
Cy Grant – Audio
Trevor Edwards – Audio
George Phillips – Audio & Film
Peter Daily – Audio & Film
Cheryl Thornley – Audio & Film
Cynthia Gittens – Audio & Film
Don Towers – Audio & Film
Kadmile McFee – Audio & Film
Trever Rochester – Audio
Peter Foster – Audio
Dennis T. Olivier – Audio - Film - Trinidad
Pirbright barracks – DART Team – Audio - Film
Lilliput Klootwijk– Holland – Audio

Other Sources

The Chaguaramas Military History & Aerospace Museum – Trinidad. Douglas Anderson – Audio
House of Commons
Encyclopedia Britannica
Charles Heath Saunders – Pirbright
Cambridge University, Wren Library
Peter Devitt – Royal Air Force Museum, Hendon
Imperial War Museum
Grant Rodgers – Imperial War Museum – Audio & Film
Garfield McFarlane – Leading Aircraftman – Audio & Film
Linda Kelshall – Military Museum – Trinidad – Audio & Film
Dennis Olivier – Aerospace Museum – Military Liaison Officer, Knight of the Museum – Audio
Clarence Thompson – Audio
Castor Williams – Audio

Published Sources – Point of Reference

Average – Trevor Edwards

The Golden One Hundred – Gaylord Kelshall

Caribbean Volunteers at War – Mark Johnson

The Story of the Second World War – Paul Dowswell

A Member of the RAF of Indeterminate Race – Cy Grant

Caribbean Wars Untold – Humphrey Metzgen – John Graham

Lancaster W4827: Failed to Return – Joost Klootwijk

The Caribbean at War – The North Kensington Archives

Barefoot Soldier – Johnson Beharry VC

Photographs

Copyright

Courtesy of the following: -

Arthur Weeks & Joseph Collins – Imperial War Museum

David Louis Clemetson – University of Cambridge, Wren Library

Alhaji Grunshi – Copyright could not be found. Artist unknown.

Ahmet Ali Celikten – Copyright could not be found.

Robinson Clarke – Origin unknown

Johnny Smythe OBE – Imperial War Museum

James Hyde – Imperial War Museum

Larry Osbourne OBE – Chaguaramas Military History & Aerospace Museum Trinidad

The Right Honorable Errol Barrow (Flight Officer) – Barbados High Commission

Philip Louie Ulric Cross DFO, DSO – Maureen Dickson

Group of Airmen – Leroy Gittens

Cy Grant's Medals – Maureen Dickson

Cy Grant's Family Photo – Sami M-Grant

Cy Grant's Jacket –Maureen Dickson

Don Towers' Book and Sketches – Jan Towers (Reed)

Basil Anderson – Chaguaramas Military History & Aerospace Museum Trinidad
Sam King – Maureen Dickson
ATS Woman – Origin unknown
Joyce Cyrus – Chaguaramas Military History & Aerospace Museum Trinidad
Cynthia Gittens – Leroy Gittens
Connie Mark, Blue Plaque – Nubian Jak
Nadia Cattouse – Collins
Collet Prince – Maureen Dickson
Cheryl Thornley – Maureen Dickson
George Phillips – George Phillips
Steve Blizzard – Steve Blizzard
Gaylord Kelshall – Linda Kelshall
Phillip Kelshall – Chaguaramas Military History & Aerospace Museum Trinidad
Leroy Gittens – Maureen Dickson
Ian Bruton – Chaguaramas Military History & Aerospace Museum Trinidad
Dennis Olivier – Dennis Olivier
Peter Daley – Peter Daley
Trevor Edwards – Trevor Edwards
Kadmile McFee – Maureen Dickson
Major Glen Lindsay – Major Lindsay
Alan Barrett – Alan Barrett
Stanley Archer – Stanley Archer
Lester Hendricks – Lester Hendricks

Johnson Beharry VC – Maureen Dickson
Today's Soldiers – Maureen Dickson
BWIR Flags – Horace Barnes – Birmingham
March Photo – Horace Barnes – Birmingham
Blue Plaque – Nubian Jak Academy

Index

Book Sleeve

Maureen Dickson formally a U.S Realtor, and TV Presenter.

Born in British Guiana (now Guyana). Grew up in England.

Maureen's long-standing passion for history took a turn after having a life-changing conversation with her now late father. Although he was too young to be in WWII, Maureen decided to look into the role of the Caribbean Volunteers. It is to this end that Maureen started to interview ex-service personnel with the aim that she would be able to preserve their war experiences for posterity, hoping that they would inspire future generations, as her father had inspired her.